D1582528

George Macaulay Trevelyan
A Portrait in Letters

THE AUTHOR

Peter Raina read Modern History at St Catherine's College, Oxford, received his MA at Clark University (USA), and his D.Phil. from the University of Warsaw. He has been a Research Fellow at the Osteuropa-Institut of the Free University Berlin, a Visiting Fellow at the Centre of International Studies, Faculty of History, Cambridge University, and at the Centre for International Studies, London School of Economics & Political Science; Research Associate, St Catherine's College, Oxford; Senior Research Associate, Graduate Centre, Balliol College, Oxford; Honorary Member of the High Table and Senior Common Room member, Christ Church, Oxford. He is a life member, Clare Hall, Cambridge.

PUBLICATIONS

In English:
Political Opposition in Poland, 1954–1977 (London: Poets & Painters Press, 1978)
Independent Social Movements in Poland (London: London School of Economics, 1981)
Poland 1981: Towards Social Renewal (London: George Allen & Unwin, 1985)
The Constitutions of New Democracies in Europe (Merlin Books, 1995)

In German:
Die Krise der Intellektuellen (Olten: Walter Verlag, 1968)
Gomulka – Politische Biographie (Köln: Verlag Wissenschaft u. Politik, 1970)
Internationale Politik in den Siebziger Jahren (Frankfurt/M: S. Fischer Verlag, 1973)

In Polish:
Kardynal Wyszynski, 8 volumes (Warsaw: von Borowiecki, 1999)
Javuzelski (Warsaw: von Borowiecki, 2001)

George
Macaulay Trevelyan

A Portrait in Letters

by
Peter Raina

Pentland Books
Edinburgh · Durham · Cambridge

First Published in 2001 by
Pentland Books
1 Hutton Close
South Church
Bishop Auckland
Durham

British Library Cataloguing in Publication Data.
A catalogue record for this book is available
from the British Library

ISBN 1 85821 958 2

Typeset by Cambridge Photosetting Services, Cambridge.
Printed and bound by Antony Rowe Ltd., Chippenham.

For Lord Alan Bullock of Leafield
and
Professor Agnes Headlam-Morley

For
Oliver

with very warm regards
Peter

Ch. Ch. Oxford
4. 09. 03

CONTENTS

Preface   ix

Early Childhood   1

At Harrow   4

At Cambridge   18

Letters to Robert Trevelyan   55

Index   159

PREFACE

George Macaulay Trevelyan[1] is perhaps one of the best known of the English historians of the last century. Born February 16 1876 at Welcombe (near Stratford-upon-Avon), the Warwickshire home of his maternal grandfather, Robert Needham Phillips, he was brought up in the family's country house at Wallington, built in beautiful Northumbria by Sir William Blacket during the reign of William III, and passed to the Trevelyans through inheritance. In later life a tireless walker, GMT developed a love of nature as a child in this Northumbrian home. His childhood was spent in an atmosphere imbued with liberal traditions, and it was in the home too that his contact with history and historians began. His father, Sir George Otto Trevelyan O.M., was both a politician and an historian, and his mother, Hannah Moore Macaulay, was the sister of Lord Macaulay, the celebrated historian. His grandfather, Sir Charles Edward Trevelyan, Indian Administrator and Head of the British Treasury, had established his reputation and career reforming the British Civil Service.

However, it was at Harrow School that his intellect and character took the form that was to determine his future career. He was deeply influenced by teachers Edward Bowen and Townsend Warner, and it was at Harrow that he learned to love poetry and to write. He won the Bourchier prize[2] for his essay on 'A Critical Estimate of the Poetry of Alfred, Lord Tennyson',[3] composed soon after the poet's death in October 1892. He observed that Tennyson's *Timbuctoo* (which had won him the Chancellor's Prize at Cambridge in 1829) was a poem 'in fine blank verse, in parts not unworthy of *Paradise Lost* ...', that the *Juvenilia*

---

1 George Macaulay Trevelyan (GMT) was the youngest of three sons of Sir George Otto Trevelyan, Bart. (1838–1928): Liberal MP (1865–86, 1887–97), Lord of the Admiralty (1868–70), Secretary to the Admiralty (1880–82), Chief Secretary for Ireland (1882), Chancellor of the Duchy of Lancaster (1884), Secretary for Scotland (1886, 1892–95); wrote *The Early History of Charles James Fox, The American Revolution* (6 volumes), *The Life and Letters of Lord Macaulay*; DCL. (Oxford,1885), O.M. (1911). The eldest son Charles Philips Trevelyan was born in 1870: ed. Harrow, Trinity Coll., Cambridge, Liberal MP (1899–1918), Labour MP (1922–31), Parliamentary Secretary to Board of Education (1908–14), President of Board of Education (1924, 1929–31), Lord-Lieut. of Northumberland (1930–49); succeeded as Bart. (1928), died 1958. The second son Robert Calverley was born in 1872. More about him later in the chapter.
2 Named in memory of E. Bourchier (Head Master 1858–63).
3 G.M. Trevelyan, 'A Critical Estimate of the Poetry of Alfred', Lord Tennyson, *Prolarsiones* (Harrow), 1893, pp. 30–44.

were 'essentially original', yet the 'metres for the most part rough, and the subject-matter crude but striking'. He found in *The Lady of Shalott* perhaps 'the most complete triumph of metre and language over the the senses that our literature affords'. It would be, he wrote, 'a mistake to praise *The May Queen*. The poem may be beautiful and pathetic, but it partakes too much of the beauty and pathos of *Lucy Gray* and *Alice Fell*. Still it is by no means true that its author falls into bathos in all his poems of homely cottage life. On the contrary, *Grandmother*, which he published in 1859, is one of the most striking and picturesque sketches of an old lady that has ever been drawn.' He argued that Tennyson was at his best in the *Morte d'Arthur*, which 'brings to perfection that descriptive art by which the poet makes the reader breathe the very atmosphere of the scene'. On the other hand, he was not much impressed by *The Princess*. Although its popularity had been secured, 'we are inclined to deny to it a place in the first rank of literary compositions, since its perfection as a work of art has been spoiled by the change of character and purpose in the latter half of the poem'.[4]

For Trevelyan, Tennyson was a remarkable poet, but, perhaps, not one of the greatest English poets, appearing 'merely to have written at the dictation of his exuberant fancy and poetical power. He is thoughtful, but not a great thinker. Apart from his literary talent, he is not above the average of cultivated Englishmen'.[5]

These lines were written by a boy who had just turned seventeen. GMT also wrote poems, two of which, both lengthy, won the school's prizes for English verse. The one on Sir John Franklin appeared in the *Harrow Journal* in 1892. The beginning lines read thus:[6]

> Proud are the tales we tell of trophies won,
> Fields fought and gained, 'neath India's scorching sun,
> Where sluggish Hoogly rolls through Plassey's plain,
> Where Sobraon's cornfields ripen o'er the slain;
> Or where the craggy cliffs of Abram fall,
> Or where the daisy grows by Goumont's wall.
> As proud our deeds in Arctic lands unknown,
> Where Solitude hath set his Northern throne

4 *Ibid.*, p. 35.
5 *Ibid.*, p. 42.
6 *Prolarsiones* (1892), p. 51.

On blocks of castled ice. His courtiers are
The cold pale moon, and every circling star;
His dome the polar sky. No voices rise;
Silence itself hath voiceless melodies;
These the sole music that the monarch hears
Through the slow rolling of the countless years.

The poem *Columbus* was published in 1893. The stanza quoted here is somewhere in the middle of the poem:[7]

Look now, Columbus, o'er the western wave!
God sees thy need, and sends you bird to save.
From out the west, on slow majestic wing
The heron comes, the gray-plumed river-king.
Oh, by what reedy pool or rushing burn
Doth his warm nest await his swift return,
In hills primeval, where a footstep rude
Hath ne'er profaned his regal solitude?
'See, see, ye cowards! banish dull despair!
Believe the sign God sends you through the air!
Whate'er the realms from whence yon heron came,
That land we call our King's, in Jesu's Name.

Great poetry became GMT's lifelong passion, influencing his style and his
imagination. But it wasn't poetry he came up to read at Trinity College,
Cambridge. He determined to study and, later, write history. He took a First
in the History Tripos of 1896, then worked on a fellowship dissertation and
soon after, in 1898, was elected Fellow of Trinity College. The dissertation was
published as *England in the Age of Wycliffe* (1899) – GMT's first book.

He married in March 1904 Janet Ward,[8] daughter of Humphry and Mary
Ward. There were three children, a daughter Mary,[9] born in 1905, a son,
Theodore, born in 1906 (died in 1911), another son, Humphry,[10] born in 1909.

7 *Prolarsiones* (1893) , p. 56.
8 Janet Penrose Trevelyan wrote *A Short History of the Italian People* (N.Y., 1920) and *The Life of Mrs. Humphry Ward* (London, 1923).
9 Mary Trevelyan married in 1930 John Moorman, afterwards Bishop of Ripon and wrote *William Wordsworth: A Biography* (1965).
10 Humphry Trevelyan became a Fellow of King's College, Cambridge and wrote *Goethe and the Greeks* (1941).

GMT's recognition as an historian was established immediately after the publication in 1907 of *Garibaldi's Defence of the Roman Republic*, first of the monumental Garibaldi trilogy. His style was criticised. The 'lights' were 'too high', wrote one critic, and the 'shadows too deep'.[11] The narrative betrayed 'Macaulayism', and the author's 'unbounded enthusiasm' for the Risorgimento had biased him against the papal policies.[12] The criticism was harsh, the judgement oversimplified.

GMT never meant to imitate Macaulay. He worked continually on his style, took great pains to polish it. He transcribed 'each paragraph four times on the average before the typing stage'.[13] He never understood the practice of history to be simply a collection and chronological display of events. Rather, history to him was both an art and a science. Historians had to be scientific, but also imaginative and literary; their role was to 'get inside the minds of the people' to 'see their problems as they saw them, not as we see them now'.[14] For him, the 'way you feel a thing is much more important than the complete truth of the thing you feel'.[15]

GMT highly valued free will, personal freedom and humanism, and for him Garibaldi symbolized all these qualities. When the remaining volumes of the trilogy appeared: *Garibaldi and the Thousand* (1909); *Garibaldi and the Making of Italy* (1911), the general public noted with satisfaction that these works were not just academic accounts of a distant man, but historical narratives written with passion and sympathy. GMT agreed that his volumes on Garibaldi were 'reeking with bias', however, as he argued,' (without) bias I should never have written them at all. For I was moved to write them by poetical sympathy with the passions of the Italian patriots of that period, which I retrospectively shared. Such merit as the work has, largely derives from that. And some of its demerits also derive from the same cause'.[16]

It would be wrong to assume that GMT overlooked 'scientific history', or failed to analyse the economic and social causes of events. His volumes of

---

11 James Tait in *English Historical Review*, No.15 (1900),161; quoted in J.M. Hernon, Jr., 'The Whig Historian and Consensus History: George Macaulay Trevelyan, 1876–1962', *American Historical Review*, No.1 (1976), p.71.

12 H. Nelson Gay in AHR,No.14 (1908–09),135; quoted in Hernon, *op. cit.*

13 G.M.Trevelyan, *An Autobiography and other Essays* (London,1949), p.1.

14 Quoted in Hernon, *op. cit.*, p.91.

15 *Ibid.*, p.72.

16 G.M.Trevelyan, *An Autobiography*, p.71.

England under Queen Anne: Blenheim (1930), *Ramillies and the Union with Scotland* (1932), *The Peace and the Protestant Succession* (1934), and later *English Social History* (1942) prove just the opposite. These works are indeed literary narratives, and equally profound in scholarly terms.

Writing about England and her statesmen, GMT gave a vivid portrait of such values as were dear to him: English liberal tradition in the *Life of John Bright* (1913), the instincts of aristocrats in *Grey of Fallodon* (1937), the temperament of the English people and the effectiveness of their political institutions in the *History of England* (1926). In the course of centuries, GMT observed, the English had formed a system, which had reconciled 'three things that other nations have often found incompatible – efficiency, popular control, and personal freedom'.[17]

GMT saw himself as an interpreter of the past; he hesitated to be an explorer of his own era: 'I don't understand the age we live in, and what I understand I don't like'.[18] Nonetheless he more than once expressed his views on the events of his times. He sympathized with the pacifist conduct of his contemporaries, but he also disagreed with them. He cared, he argued, '*much* more about individual freedom as the precondition of good civilization than about anything else in politics and society'. He had 'the most extraordinary good luck in life' and if 'I have availed myself of my chances well, it is partly because I have not gone in for the rough and tumble of the world's debate. I think I was right, as my gifts were literary, not administrative or political. But no one knows better than I do that I am no hero'.[19]

Such was his modest opinion of himself. Others judged him differently. For his gallant services as the commandant of a Red Cross Field Ambulance during the First World War in Italy, GMT was awarded the Italian Silver Medal for Valour, in England the C.B.E. His appointment in 1927 as the Regius Professor of Modern History at Cambridge resulted from the knowledge that he was one of the leading historians of his country. The bestowal of the Order of Merit in 1930 justified the personal distinction of the historian. In the autumn of 1940 the Mastership of Trinity College Cambridge falling vacant, the Prime Minister, Winston Churchill, asked the King to appoint GMT as Master of the College. He retired from Mastership in 1951. During this period, he also chaired the

17 G.M. Trevelyan, *History of England* (London, 1926), xvii.
18 GMT in a letter dated 27 October 1926 to his brother Robert.
19 Quoted in Hernon, *op. cit.*, p. 87.

executive committee of the National Trust and accepted responsibilities in Trusteeship of the British Museum and of the National Portrait Gallery. George Macaulay Trevelyan died at his home in Cambridge on 20 July 1962, at the age of 86. *The Times'* deservedly long obituary ended thus: 'He will be remembered no less as a great Englishman, one who consecrated an individual genius to preserving the best of our English heritage, to continuing and developing a high national tradition of literary history, and to making it acceptable to a new age'.[20]

GMT was an eager correspondent as well; never tired of writing letters, both public and private. There are hundreds of them. But it is his private correspondence which concerns us here. He wrote often to his brothers, Charles and Robert. Many of his letters to Charles have been made public by Mary Moorman in her *George Macaulay Trevelyan: A Memoir by her Daughter* (Hamish Hamilton: London 1980) and by David Cannadine in his full length biography of the historian: *G.M. Trevelyan: A Life in History* (Harper Collins: London 1992). On the other hand very few letters written by GMT to his brother Robert have been published. In this volume are printed most of these letters, which are thus available to the public for the first time.

Robert Calverley Trevelyan (Bob) was born on 28 June 1872. After leaving Harrow he read classics at Trinity College, Cambridge. He became a poet and a translator of classic Greek and Latin literature. His first volume of poetry, *Mallow and Asphodel* appeared in 1898. Bob wrote fables (*Sisyphus*), opera texts (*The Bride of Dionysus*, for which Donald Tovey composed music), and various dramatic and satirical poems. Bob was married in 1900 to a Dutch lady, Elizabeth van der Hoeven. They had one son, Julian, the painter.[21] Robert C. Trevelyan died on 21 March 1951.

In a brief but excellent essay on The Master of Trinity College, Cambridge, Lord Humphrey Trevelyan[22] (no relation) wrote some time ago that GMT's letters 'display the generosity and sympathy of his mind and help to illuminate his character. Moreover, he was a natural writer and they are often a delight to read.'[23] The present volume may well justify the point. To Bob, GMT confided

---

20 *Obituaries from The Times, 1961–1970* (Reading, 1975), p.796.
21 The elder son, Paul, died early in his childhood. Julian Otto Trevelyan (1910-88) became known for his surrealist and expressionist style, his painting indicating fantasy and style.
22 Humphrey Trevelyan (1905–85), senior civil servant and diplomat: HM Chargé d'Affaires in Peking (1953–55), Ambassador to Egypt (1955–56), Iraq (1958–61), the USSR (1962–65).
23 Humphrey Trevelyan, *Public and Private* (London,1980), p.149.

his wishes, feelings and opinions from the early days of boyhood, through the years of maturity and until Bob's death. The two brothers had much in common. GMT loved poetry, and classical literature. Bob was a poet, and a translator of the classics. GMT was an admirer of Bob's works. David Cannadine is quite unfair in stating that Robert Trevelyan 'spent his life time writing undistinguished poetry'.[24] Bob's poetry has been more accurately judged by Desmond MacCarthy, a master critic and master judge of the literature of his times. 'The force and exactness of his diction is unobtrusive',[25] he said of Robert Trevelyan. 'His work has a classical air; and not the least charm of his poetry is that a whimsical fancy often finds in it unerring, conservative expression.'[26] It 'was not urgency of emotion or the feeling that his emotions were better than other men's which first drew him to poetry, but the unexhaustible delight of form'.[27] 'His masters have been the classic poets who have taught him the art of reserve and the sufficiency of flawless statement.'[28] It is true that Robert Trevelyan was better noted for his translations than his own verse. 'I think,' writes Desmond MacCarthy, '(it was Robert's) devotion to the classics which limited his audience. It was the source of his own excellence, yet it checked his originality, which, as here and there his poems have shown, was in the direction of a humorous charm; and it separated him from his time.'[29]

Whatever might be the literary value of Bob's works GMT welcomed everything that Bob wrote. He thought so highly of Bob's accomplishments that he sent his own historical writings to his brother, so that the poet could polish the style and the diction of the historian.

Perhaps the exchange of the letters between the poet and the historian at the start of World War I is of the greatest interest. But what about other letters? Are they then simply trivial? Some are indeed scrappy; others, perhaps, repetitive. But there is GMT's soul in all of them. They display his character – his ethical faith, his uncompromising honesty, his humour, his indignation at things unjust, his love for liberty, truth, fairness and beauty. GMT might lose his temper, but

24 David Cannadine, *G.M. Trevelyan: A Life in History* (London, 1992), p. 13.
25 Desmond MacCarthy quoted in : R.C. Trevelyan, *Selected Poems* (edited by Humphry Trevelyan), London, 1953, p. viii.
26 *Ibid.*
27 *Ibid.*
28 *Ibid.*, p.ix.
29 *Ibid.*, pp.xii–xiii.

he is not malicious, never cynical. There is always something to stand for, even if it is only pure, noble, aesthetic, honourable.

GMT's letters to Bob and to Bessie (Bob's wife) are in the care of Trinity College Library, Cambridge. They are catalogued under RCT Papers. In tracing them I was greatly helped by Dr Philip Gaskell formerly Librarian and by late Dr Robert Robson, Fellow of Trinity College, Cambridge. I am grateful to the Master and Fellows of Trinity College Cambridge for making these letters accessible to me, and to the present Librarian, Dr David McKitterick for his assistance. The copyright is owned by GMT's grandson, the present George Macaulay Trevelyan. I have sought and obtained Mr Trevelyan's permission for the publication of the material published in this volume. And I am indeed grateful to Mr G.M. Trevelyan for granting me this permission. My thanks are due to Mr Peter Hunter, Librarian, Harrow School, for his help in my research, and to late Mr A.L. Rowse and Mr Raleigh Trevelyan for their comments.

PETER RAINA

Early Childhood

George Macaulay Trevelyan had barely turned six when, during his stay with his father, Sir George Otto Trevelyan, in Ireland, he felt 'unconsciously a sense of the drama of English and Irish history was purveyed to me through daily sights and experiences with my father as commentator and bard'.[1] Sir George had been sent to Ireland in 1882 as Chief Secretary, and he had taken along with him the youngest of his three sons. The young George spent much of his time 'wandering round the wooded circle of the Chief Secretary's grounds'.[2] Here the boy was strictly guarded lest he be kidnapped or harmed otherwise by the Irish nationalists. Thus it was in Ireland that the 'love of history was deeply and affectionately planted in me while living thus, a queer, happy little boy, almost alone with my parents in this oasis in the surrounding prairie of the Phoenix'.[3] George was alone because his two elder brothers, Charles and Robert, were at school.

Sir George returned to England in 1884 and took residence in London, at 40 Ennismore Gardens, S.W. One of GMT's earliest letters is addressed to his brother Robert from his London home:

> Dear Bobbie,
> Aunt Meggie has given me an ornament shelf and I have put your carving out of the glass table on it and mine too, do you mind?
> I am getting on well, and I hope you are too. I have begun to read Josef, and find it very nice. All send love.
> Georgie.

At the age of eight GMT was sent off to a private boarding school at Wixenford 'on the borders of Berkshire and Hampshire, amid pinewoods and heaths...'[4] The quiet and beautiful countryside was to the young boy's taste. Here he got the first pleasures of solitary walking and he learnt to be 'walker-alone' - later to become GMT's lifelong hobby. At Wixendorf, the headmaster, E.P. Arnold, drilled George in Latin Prose. George, however, doubted if he would ever

---

1 G.M. Trevelyan, *An Autobiography & other Essays* (Longmans:London,1949), p.7.
2 *Ibid.*
3 *Ibid.*
4 *Ibid.*, p.8.

become a classics scholar. Nor did he ever dream of 'being a general, or a states-man or an engine-driver, like other aspiring children'.[5] George liked poetry very much, read a lot of it and thought he 'might possibly be a poet!' Above all he desired to be an historian.

GMT's first contact with serious literature began at the age of 11 when he received Percy's *Reliques of Ancient Poetry* as a prize awarded for industry in Greek, History, French and Mathematics at the end of his second year at the Wixenford school. During the Easter holidays of 1888 GMT 'got a fit of Shakespeare' and devoured *Henry V*, *King John* and *Henry IV*. In the following summer he read 'a great deal' of Macaulay.

> It was very wet on Thursday and Friday, but it was not at all dull, for I was reading Macaulay. I have read a great deal now and am very interested in it … how I do wish he had lived long enough to write Anne's reign, but perhaps if there was more of it, the last part would be not so good, but it was impossible for Macaulay to write anything uninterest-ing.[6]

Macaulay had received priority not only because it would be obligatory for any future historian to read him, but also because GMT's father, Sir George, had himself written a fascinating *Life of Macaulay*.

At Wixenford GMT found most boys and all the masters 'bigotted conserva-tives'.[7] George was being brought up in liberal thinking at home. At school there were not many with whom he could debate openly. His 'two best friends' were Will Finlay and Hugh Law,' the dear impulsive Irishman'.[8] GMT made no secret of his sympathies towards the Irish cause, a topic current at the time. The imprisonment of the Irish members deeply distressed him.

> What a comfort and consolation it must be to those poor members in their cells to know that they are suffering in a good cause, and that so many sympathise with them. One of the psalms today was *Why boastest thou thyself thou tyrant*.

---

5 *Ibid.*, p.9.
6 Quoted in Mary Moorman, 'The Youth of an Historian: George Macaulay Trevelyan', *Contemporary Review*, vol. 224 (1974), p. 300.
7 *Ibid.*, p. 299
8 G.M. Trevelyan, *op. cit.*, p. 8.

I am sure such tyranny cannot last for long, for no tyranny ever did last, much less in a civilised christian country like Great Britain …[9]

Not many boys thought likewise.

9 Mary Moorman, *op. cit*, p. 299.

At Harrow

The disappointment with the way that his contemporaries thought was the greater when GMT came to Harrow in September 1889. In those days Harrow housed about 600 boys, mostly from the English country gentlemen and the Victorian business class. The boys were generally prepared to take over business from their parents, to join the Army or the Civil Service. Sports formed the most popular discipline among the boys. GMT found himself 'a misfit at Harrow', 'a complete muff at Cricket, and clumsy at football', though he liked it.[1] George stayed at the Grove (the same house where his brother, Robert, had lodged), of which Edward Bowen★ (an old friend of Sir George's) was the master. George got along quite well with the head of the house, Richard Sandilands†,' a king among boys'. Outside his own house his close friends included Philip Wilbraham Baker‡ and Charles Roden Buxton§. If the number of desired friends was not satisfactory, then at least GMT seems to be grateful to have 'remarkable' masters at Harrow, from whom he 'gained much both in and out of school'. They encouraged his 'literary tastes and pruned' his 'exuberant English prose'.[2] And 'thanks largely to them', he had 'no lack of literary talk and discussion for which I craved'.[3] He was further lucky to have been tutored by 'two history masters of rare quality - Robert Somervell and George Townsend Warner'. GMT had no doubt that at Harrow he had 'a better historical education than any other school boy in England'.[4] The headmaster of Harrow, J.E.C. Welldon, had also noted how keenly George Trevelyan was interested in history, and for this purpose the headmaster 'most wisely' handed George over to Warner 'as his private pupil' during George's last year at Harrow. GMT gorged himself on Gibbon, Macaulay, Carlyle and Stubbs' *Constitutional History*. But equally he read poetry 'with passionate delight'.[5] Shakespeare, Milton, Shelley, Keats, Tennyson meant to GMT quite as much as Gibbon or Macaulay. The English poets, records

★Edward Ernest Bowen, Assistant Master 1859–1901, Housemaster at the Grove 1881–1901. He was also a fanatical walker.

†Harold Richard Sandilands (The Grove). Left 1894. Trin. Coll. Camb.; served in Boer War; D.S.O. Great War, 1914-18; Brigadier; C.M.G.

‡Philip Wilbraham Baker (The Knoll). Monitor 1891; Head of the School, 1893; Leaf Scholar, 1894; left 1894. ed. Balliol Coll. Oxf.; Fellow of All Souls, 1899. Barrister, 1901. Chancellor, Dio. of Chester, 1913–34. D.C.L. Lambeth.

§Charles Roden Buxton (Small Houses). Monitor, 1892; left 1894; Trin. Coll. Camb. Barrister, 1902; MP 1910; author of *Turkey in Revolution*. MP 1922-3.

GMT, 'have supplied me throughout my life with the sacred books of my eclectic philosophy and religion. Love of poetry has affected the character, and in places the style of my historical writings, and in part dictated my choice of subjects'.[6]

Life at Harrow must have been a little lonely for GMT. 'I find that the only way to get along here', he wrote to his mother in May 1893, 'is to be engaged vigorously all day at some literary, political or historical study. I am throwing myself into history with a vigour that I never knew myself capable of before'.[7]

To Robert he posted the following letter:

Spider and Spot alright. Took	The Grove,
former back to Mrs Webster.	Harrow.
Webster getting very slowly	Jan. 29. Friday.
better after a relapse.	

Dear Bobbie

I am writing to you from want of anything better to do, so do not trouble to write back. We had a very pleasant week at Wallington, and I went to see Aunt Annie★ on Tuesday morning and spent the night there, and saw Miss Martin† on Wednesday before I came back.

I found Sophie much more cheerful and talkative than I expected, and altogether enjoyed myself very much there. The losses in the battle‡ were nearly equal. You lost 417 and I lost 391. I found Kellerman among the dead. The red Yng. Grd. lost over 100 which I should think was the record, as only 5 of them were prisoners.

The regiment itself is now over 200. The Prussians lost over 90 which is almost more severe in proportion to the regiment. Lady Frederick

★Anna Maria Philips (GMT's mother's sister) was 'the beloved and ever-welcome aunt and great-aunt of the next two generations of Trevelyans' – wrote GMT's daughter Mary Moorman in her 'The Youth of an Historian: George Macaulay Trevelyan', *Contemporary Review*, Vol. 224 (1974), p .248.

†Miss Martin was GMT's private tutor before he was sent to Wixenford preparatory school in Hampshire in 1885.

‡The favourite pastime of all three brothers at Wallington had been war-game, played with armies of small soldiers. Here is how Robert describes it: 'A large space of bare floor boards in my bedroom and afterwards in the museum (a spacious attic in which many early natural history collections were housed), was kept for military purposes, and there many hours would be spent in arranging the English and French armies (each nearly 2000 men strong), and manipulating their conflicts. The battles were Napoleonic in character … As there were three of us, two could command the armies of Wellington or Napoleon, while the third could act the part of impartial Destiny, receiving from time to time secret instructions from the opposing generals … and deciding how many and which soldiers should be killed and wounded, and knocking them over one by one with his finger … A battle would often take weeks of hard work and had sometimes to be left unfinished at the end of the holidays. But it was a wonderful game, and we continued playing it right down to our undergraduate days and even for some years later'. Quoted in Mary Moorman, *Ibid.*, p.248.

Cavendish will be at Wallington by this time, where she is going to spend a few days.

Here very few people have left this term in the school, though several in the house.

Clive has managed to skew his Sandhurst exams, and has come back as a pleasant surprise. He has of course got this corridor instead of me.

The finds have been arranged very satisfactorily. Clive and Sandilands find together, and Farquhar§ and Tregoning¶ and I find together in Tregoning's room (the library) in the morning, and for tea Farquhar and I find in my room, and Tregoning alone in his.

I have to read prayers now. Welldon is such a terrible funk of the influenza that some changes too horrible for relation have been introduced, but happily only for the time till the weather gets better.

HAVE NO FIRST SCHOOL AND ONLY ONE HALF HOLIDAY A WEEK.

WE HAVE A BIT OF FIRST SCHOOL SHOVED IN BETWEEN DINNER AND LUNCHEON.

WE ALL HAVE TO WEAR SWEATERS for going down to footer in. There is no word in the English language to express my abhorrence of it all. I perfectly sympathize with all conservatives in every age and place. Of course the result is that we are working all day between breakfast and tea.

I hope we shall all get the influenza and die of it to pay Welldon out.

I suppose however it will not last longer than for a few weeks.

Yrs affectly,
G.M. Trevelyan.

Some of the boys indeed irritated him at the school. Once one of them said to him on the day before the Derby that he didn't suppose 'you even know the name of the favourite'. George was enraged: these 'aristocratic curs'. Wait, he recorded, 'till I grow up and my brain and pen which you despise so, or you and your horses and cricket-bats will win the battle of life'.[8] George spent his spare

§Hobart Brooks Farquhar (The Grove). Left 1892. Trin. Coll. Camb.; served in Boer War; Great War; killed in action at Vimy Ridge, 22 May 1916.
¶Arthur Langford Tregoning (The Grove). Left 1893. Trin. Coll. Camb., B.A. 1896; M.A. 1910.

time in devouring books and reading newspapers. He preferred Shelley to Byron. Shelley's poetry, he thought, was of an 'absolutely different and higher order' and it made George feel 'bowed down and humbled'. Reading *Don Juan* was indeed 'great fun', but 'that God's poets are no longer allowed to waste their powers on such beastliness'.[9]... Tennyson became the favourite. GMT read Pepys' diary almost 'every evening just as a better Christian reads his chapter of the bible'.[10] Ruskin's *Modern Painters* and *The Stones of Venice* opened new fields of interest. Of A.M.Sullivan's *New Ireland*, he wrote that he had 'never read a book with such devouring eagerness since I finished Renan's *Vie de Jésus*'.[11] The liberal *Daily Chronicle* and *Westminster Gazette* were regularly read. There was also time enough to update his brother, Robert, on what was going on at Harrow:

The Grove,
Harrow on the Hill.
Sept. 20, 1891.

Dear Bobbie,

I am not going to write to Papa or Mama today, but you can tell them anything they want to know from this letter. I have got three photographs from Hills and Saunder's, and gave one to Tom, and one to Moss, who I found in a very cosy little study, much like his old one.

He has already made himself popular in the house by introducing several commonsense reforms, which Farquhar was too old to see the need of. Stow★ says Bentinck is getting along but is rather too retiring. I do not know anything about the new books yet.

Gilmore has grown a beard. I saw Hicks[†] in chapel today, but nowhere else.

Fourth form bill has been abolished, because of the row last term. I suppose you will think it a great shame, but I must say I think it was a very slow stupid business. One reform, however, I am sure you will approve of, that is that instead of doing Greek test the whole sixth is going to do old test history out of the English Bible, but I am afraid it is likely to be only for one or two terms.

I got my remove, rather to my surprise, and there were not very many removes.

Stow and I sit at that separate desk for two at Welldon's left flank. I swot with Elliott;[‡] which makes the cons very much easier; and altogether I dare say I shall not have much more work than last term, especially as I get off verse and several other disagreeable institutions. Elliott has your old room.

It is not impossible that I may have it next term, or at any rate pretty soon, because there is going to be a tremendous clearance at the end of the term, for Clive Booth and Elliott are certainly leaving, and Farquhar probably. I own, however, that I do not expect Mo will let them all go. The house is immensely changed this term, and a large number of people, including myself, seem to

---

★Arthur Rigby Stow (Small Houses). Left 1891. Late Member of the London Stock Exchange.
[†]Frederick Cyril Hicks (The Head Master's). Monitor, 1888; Head of the School, 1890; Balliol Coll. Oxf.; ordained 1897; Bishop of Lincoln, 1933; Governor of the School, 1927; Visitor of Eton College and King's College, Camb.; and of Lincoln Coll. Oxf.
[‡]Edward Hugh Elliott; left Harrow 1893; served in Boer War in West Africa; Great War (1914–18); *Croix de Guerre* (France) 1916.

be much more important. I think I shall enjoy this next year very much. Sandilands is a capital head. He and Rome★ are going to join the Corps, but Tom is not, I suppose a great deal because he is leaving this term. I have unfortunately told Hills and Saunders to send the rest of the photos and the bill to Trinity instead of Wallington, and was too slack to go up yesterday to tell them right. Possibly they have not yet sent them, in which case I will tell them tomorrow, but if they have sent them, I will send a postcard to tell you, and you can write to Cambridge to have them sent on.

I will now explain to you about the finds. Clive and Farquhar of course find together, and there is not room for a third in the room, even if they wanted one.

Sandilands, Tom and Elliott wanted to find together in no. 20. Tregoning got into the 6th, and the duty of finding with him devolved on me, as I got into the upper-sixth.

I immediately told Sandilands I did not want to, and he referred me to Mo. I told Mo I wanted to go on in Hall. Mo said I had a perfect right to if I chose, and seemed to sympathize with me.

So I thought it would be all right and that I should be quite happy in Hall with people like young Sandilands and such-like, and I knew Tregoning would be quite contented to find alone.

This was of course the natural and the only rational way in which the affair would have been settled in any other house, but suddenly Sandilands came into my room and said that Mo would not allow Tregoning to find alone, and that if I went downstairs, Elliott would have to find with him. I had a right to go down if I liked, but this of course was different, and I felt that if it was a matter of either Elliott or myself finding with him, I must accept. For it would be very rough on El to have to do so his last term and being a monitor. After all I have plenty more terms after this to find in, and it would have been selfish to say anything more; so I and Tregoning find in my room.

He does whatever I like, and does not make himself at all objectionable, but I shall be most heartily sick of him by the end of the term.

I hope you have not found this story too long, but I thought you would like to have an exact explanation of the case. El leaves for India in the first week of the hols, and is going to wander about the country with a tutor, under the

---

★Claud Stuart Rome (The Grove). Left 1893; joined 11th Hussars,1895; served in Boer War; Great War, 1914–18; D.S.0. 1918; C.M.G.; General. Assistant Master at Harrow, 1899–1929; Housemaster at Church Hill, 1912–15 and at the Grove, 1915–29.

impression he is going to do a lot of swot there; I told him I did not expect he would do any at all.

Tom is going to try to go to Trinity for a year or so, before entering business. Rothschild has come this term to the house, but he has to conform, and will be allowed to eat the breakfast cold ham, which is one of the advantages of Christianity.

As to our footer, one cannot say yet very much. We have had some very good games, especially as the rain has prevented Rome being carried off to play cricket. Elliott is playing back very well, and I should think very likely either Pope or M-Bar. will be played forward. I do not know about Rome or Sand playing side, as there are a good lot of people who want to be sides i.e. Clive, Bradley*, Picky and young Sandilands, who are all fair.

By the way, the 'sporting element' is completely suppressed, and Lefrez is quite a fish out of water.

I was telling young Sandilands our adventures in the Balmoral, and directly I mentioned that we had met a cracky sort of man there he immediately asked if his name was Haddock. He apparently stopped a night there a year ago, and he pounced on them and did exactly the same to them, leaving an impression not effaced by a year.

Yrs affectionately

G.M. Trevelyan.

GMT was now getting tired of what he described as 'uncongenial clime' at Harrow.[12] He wrote to his father in summer 1893 that he wanted to 'get into a world where the bat and the betting-book are not mightier than the pen and the poem'.[13] He felt 'gagged' at Harrow. He had an urgent desire to be at the disposal of a common man, whom he loved. In a letter to his eldest brother, Charles, GMT wrote that if he 'can ever do anything for democracy, it must be through literature. Now the point is that literary people are not, most of them, democratic, and it is more than probable that unless I keep the fire ever kindled within me, I shall soon forget my 'motif', and become a mere 'litterateur'! What excited aversion was the hypocrisy that surrounded him. He refused to contribute to a wedding gift which his school was to present to the Duke of

---

*Robert William Bradley (The Grove). Left 1892. Served in Boer War; D.S.O. 1902; Great War, Lieut.-Col. M.G.C., 1914-17.

11

York (afterwards King George V) on his marriage to Princess Mary. 'My money can be better spent,' recorded GMT. 'It is right that this aristocratic school should give her something, but I am the democratic exception in this high class establishment. It is curious that whereas everybody I speak to, Master or boy, says in so many words "What beastly rot the wedding present is", no one except myself has had the ordinary moral courage, or rather common sense, not to give anything. They have got a clock that everyone admits looks as if it cost £10, but which on account of its inside really costs £120 ... Now why in the name of all that is useful, couldn't they have got a £10 clock, and given £110 in the name of the Duke of York to some charitable institution? O horrible abuse of utilitarianism! Everybody admits it would have been more sensible, but nobody does it!'[15]

Equally uncompromising were GMT's views on Christianity. To him the only person who represented the spirit of true Christianity was St. Francis of Assisi - 'a true *democrat* in the highest sense of the word - the first person since Christ was crucified who *really* understood that true Christianity was the Gospel of the poor'. Jessop's *Coming of the Friars* had considerably influenced GMT's views. Christianity might still help the people, if it were preached as its Founder had intended. The progress of the human race was the only thing that GMT could 'believe in for certain'. 'What people usually call religion, the immortality of the soul and so on, I am in absolute darkness and doubt about those things. But in democracy I have got hold of something definite'.[16] Democracy was 'all in all my religion, whereby I live and move and have my being ... Democracy is I think the corollary of the teaching of Christ.'[17]

The everyday life at the school went on as usual, of which Robert was fully informed:

The Grove,
Harrow.
Sunday. Feb. 2.

Dear Bobby,

Thanks for your letter. Chatham thinks the balls would travel safest unblown. We have just had a thaw last night, after a few days skating on the much vexed pond. Bowen lost his case last holidays, but has had a triumph this term which has more than consoled him. The son of Belial who has been his chief enemy throughout, tried to come into the Grove about a fortnight ago to see that the pond was all right. Bowen promptly turned him off the premises, and told him that if he came back he would prosecute him for trespass. The baffled son of Belial accordingly appealed for protection to a magistrate, who very properly decided in Bowen's favour, and forbade the S. of B. to go into the Grove. This triumph has proved ample compensation to Bowen for losing his case.

We shall only be average at torpids; old Harre is coming on tremendously as a back.

There have been no rows in the house, and only one in the school, which was that Welldon found Crofton and Wilson and a few others having a boxing match *on Sunday* last, at which you may imagine he was most terrible in his righteous wrath. There is however nothing much to tell you, except that a rumour has been started in the school that Bowen (E.E.) is going to stand for Leeds at the next general election.

Its only foundation is a paragraph in the *Harrow Gazette*, and is easily accounted for, because he *was* going to have stood for Leeds somewhere back in 1885.

I have been shewing Bible [...] lately (N.B. Since you have left we have relapsed into epistles again, and no second Judge has arisen to deliver Israel) and with a religious bigotry worthy of Ignatius Loyola or Bishop Bonner, Welldon makes me write out 62 verses every Sunday. I can think of nothing worth writing about.

So far from being redeemed from a career of vice, Clive's military ardour has only been heated by this first repulse, and he returns to the attack in June next, and is meanwhile busily employed in mobilization. He comes to Charter's lectures now with me, and appreciates them more than most of the audience.

We are doing the constitution from 1689–1760 this term.

Your affectionate
brother
G.M. Trevelyan.

On occasions GMT sought Robert's advice on how he should cope with his school work:

Dear Bob,

I hear you are going abroad on Saturday.

I hope you will enjoy yourself. By the way, who are you going with?

How soon shall we hear about your degree?

There are one or two things which I thought you might write to tell me before you go abroad.

1. Have I to pass *again* in elementary mathematics in October? I am going, of course, to take up French instead of *higher* mathematics, but I believe I have anyhow got to pass again in elementary.
2. Is the French very easy, and with what degree of care is it necessary to do the books we have to read for it? I believe they are some plays of Corneille.
3. I suppose the Paley only takes a few days to get up with the help of a Paley-card.

I hope I shall see plenty of you at Wallington in August and September, but I suppose I shall not see you at Harrow before you go off. If you do come down, we shall have lots to talk about.,

I am enjoying this term in a way I never enjoyed Harrow before. With plenty of friends, or at least acquaintances, and no fear of surviving them next term, there is nothing in my position that I would have changed.

I am enjoying getting up the acting and spouting for Speech Day with Baker and Geikie★, and I am working at history even harder than I was at the beginning of the term. At the same time I have plenty of time for reading.

We have great fun at second XIs. Young Sandilands plays there, and they are all rather a nice set. I doubt if I would change it for Ist Vth company, even if I was good enough. If there is any possibility of your coming down before you go abroad, do come. I don't feel as if I saw you at all, last time.

Your affectionate brother,

G.M. Trevelyan.

P.S. How about this row of old bags?

★Roderick Geikie (H.B. and Mr. Marshall's). Monitor, 1890; Head of the School, 1892; left 1893; King's Coll. Camb.; Fellow of King's Coll. 1900. Killed by a train, 1910.

Other experiences, though trifles, GMT couldn't keep to himself. He wanted to share them with his brother, perhaps to refresh Robert's own memories.

Dear Bob,

Arma virumque cano!

Act I

On Tuesday after bill, 4 Vannites walked down the Foss from the bill yard to their new house. Sandilands and Rome, returning together, see them, make for them, knock one down, put another over the wall, and the rest go off without fighting. This is only one incident in the fight. There were 100 such, for by this time our men lower down in the school came rushing up from bill, and though still outnumbered we were no longer 1 to 3. The top of the Foss now became a surging mass of dust and struggling boys (some 50 in all), while Dones yelled for Van's from below and Mosses and half the rest of the school bawled for us, standing in a dense crowd by the church yard.

We fought for 10 minutes, and then mutually exhausted, parted. They walked down the Foss, as the only way out of it, and we went home.

Act II

After Bill *today*, Thursday, Rome, Sandilands, self, Tregoning and Crowdy★ (i.e. the 6th form) wait at the top of the Foss after bill.

A body of 20 Vannites advances, composed of their sixth form en masse and many others. We challenge them and fight. They are (at first) three to one, as they admit themselves. We are each seized by three or more men, and Rome and Crowdy and myself put over the wall after a violent tussle, I taking with me one man and Rome another or more, he being set on by at least six men, I by three. It was very exciting at one moment, as I hung over the wall, feeling I must go, but determined to take one of my assailants with me. I had him round the neck, and so hung for quite a quarter of a minute, when he suddenly gave a shriek and for fear of falling on his head, kicked his legs over, and over the wall we went together into a bush.

★James Crowdy (The Grove). Left 1894. Trin. Coll. Camb.; Canadian Civil Service, 1906; Deputy of the Secretary of the Governor-General of Canada, 1923; M.V.O., 1916.

Act III

8.15 p.m. I went into Bowen's study and, in answer to his enquiry, said I *was* in the row. Sandilands had just come out when I went in to his study. The rest of the dim future hides.

Floreat Nemius?

9.15. At prayers we were directed to come down to Hall again in ten minutes to hear our sentence or be jawed.

Lord knows what's going to happen. I suppose that personally, being degered from being a monitor, is the least I can expect.

If I have time I will add what Mo says to us after we have come up again.

I feel in exuberant spirits, as does everybody. You see the Grovites have still something left in them. We have offered to fight them on fair terms, that is equal numbers, but I should think the beaks will have stopped all that sort of thing before tomorrow.

I have just come up from Hall. Mo has said just what I thought, dwelt on his own sacrifices for the house (of which I know more than most boys) and the bitterness of his disappointment.

It really touched me, it is the one thing that grieves me in the business.

It is certain I shall be [...], I should think, as he said the older boys would be punished. What will happen to Sandilands, the most criminal of all, it is hard to say.

GMT's last year at Harrow (1892–93) was the happiest. But when asked by his father in the summer of 1893 whether he would want to stay on another full year at the school GMT wrote back that another term 'would sicken me; another year drive me into open revolt'. He now wished to 'get into a world when the bat and the betting-book are not mightier than the pen and the poem'. Later that year GMT was admitted to Trinity College, Cambridge. He was seventeen then.

Notes
1 G.M. Trevelyan, *An Autobiography, op cit.*, p. 9.
2 *Ibid.*, p. 10.
3 *Ibid.*,
4 *Ibid.*, p. 11.

5 *Ibid.*, p. 12
6 *Ibid.*, p.12–13.
7 Quoted in Mary Moorman, Last Years at Harrow, *Contemporary Review*, vol. 225 (1974), p. 14.
8 *Ibid.*
9 *Ibid.*
10 *Ibid.*, p.15.
11 *Ibid.*, p. 14.
12 *Ibid.*, p. 15.
13 *Ibid.*
14 *Ibid.*, p. 16.
15 *Ibid.*
16 *Ibid.*
17 GMT to his brother Charles Philip Trevelyan, 19 July 1893. Quoted in Joseph M. Hernon, Jr., 'The Last Whig Historian and Consensus History: George Macaulay Trevelyan, 1876–1962' *The American Historical Review*, No. 1, February 1976, p. 69.
18 Mary Moorman, *Last Years at Harrow, op cit.*, p. 16.

At Cambridge

When GMT arrived in Cambridge in October 1893 he felt lonely. 'I shall not feel safe till I have a *friend* here'.[1] Very soon, however, he made 'an immense number of delightful acquaintances'.[2] These were what became very distinguished men of letters later: G.E. Moore,[3] Bertrand Russel',[4] Alfred Whitehead,[5] Ralph Vaughan Williams,[6] Maurice Amos,[7] Desmond MacCarthy,[8] G.P. Gooch,[9] Ralph Wedgwood[10] and Frederic Maitland.[11] GMT could now hardly complain that he was either 'a misfit' socially or had no one worthwhile to talk to. He read 'endless books and essays', more poetry than history. He came, as he later wrote, 'under the spell of Swinburne and Browning, and made the rarer discovery of George Meredith's poems for myself. In fact the English poets have supplied me throughout my life with the sacred books of my eclectic philosophy and religion. Love of poetry has affected the character, and in places the style of my historical writings ...'.[12]

1 Mary Moorman, 'The Youth of an Historian: George Macaulay Trevelyan', *Contemporary Review*, vol. 225 (1974), p. 90.
2 *Ibid.*
3 George Edward Moore (1873–1958); leading 20th century British philosopher; classical tripos, Trin. Coll. Camb.,1894; editor of *Mind*, 1921–47; major work: *Principia Ethica*,1903.
4 Bertrand Russell (1872–1970); philosopher and social reformer; O.M.,1949; Nobel Prize for literature,1950.
5 Alfred North Whitehead (1861–1947); leading mathematician and philosopher; Fellow of Trin. Coll., Camb.,1884-1947. Major work (with Bertrand Russell) *Principia Mathematica*, 1910–13.
6 Ralph Vaughan Williams (1872–1958); leading British composer; works include symphonies 'Pastoral',1922,'Sinfonia Antarctica', 1952.
7 Sir Maurice Amos (1872–1940); moral sciences tripos, Trin. Coll. Camb.,1895; judge in Egypt,1903–12; judicial adviser, Egyptian goverment,1917–25; professor of comparative law, London,1932-7.
8 Sir Charles Otto Desmond MacCarthy (1877–1952); leading literary and dramatic critic; literary editor of *New Statesman*,1920-7; of the *Sunday Times*,1928.
9 George Peabody Gooch (1873–1968); historian; major works: *History and Historians in the Nineteenth Century*, 1913; joint editor: *Cambridge History of British Foreign policy*,1922–3; *British Documents on the Origins of the War*, 13 vols,1926–38.
10 Sir Ralph Lewis Wedgwood (1874–1956); modernized British Railways. His daughter Veronica achieved distinction as an historian.
11 Frederic Maitland (1850–1906); moral science tripos, Trin. Coll. Camb.,1872; Downing Professor of the Laws of England at Cambridge,1888–1906; major work: *The Constitutional History of England*, 1908.
12 G.M. Trevelyan, *An Autobiography, op. cit*, pp.11–12.

Of his life in Cambridge, his excursions in the countryside, his travels abroad GMT communicated to his brother Robert.

Here is how he spent his time travelling with his friends in the mountains, also visiting places where Wordsworth lived. GMT never had a 'jollier time'.

April 5. [1895]
Seatoller.

Dear Bob,

Though you are no doubt enjoying yourself very much, getting warmth without wraps and beauty without books still you may feel a long way from England and be glad of a letter in the tongue of your fathers. Amos and Wedgwood and Moore and I are here, Vaughan Williams having left a few days ago. The weather has turned better in the last few days and we are having a splendid time of it. Wedgwood and I bathe in Cambridge pool every morning, then we work in the morning, Amos and Wedgwood, who are taking their Triposes very hard – 7 hours a day, and Moore reading *Jane Eyre* and novels chiefly, and I all sorts of jolly books, some connected with history and some not, but none tripos work. I never had a jollier time. The party suits itself very well; we get on splendidly; it is even a greater success than the Skye party. There is not the slight distance between Moore and Wedgwood that there was at Skye. We scramble on the mountains in the afternoon, not generally going far or on great heights, the top mountains being glacial – very fine and beautiful but cold and bad for climbing. I have however been over Great Gable and so down to Ennerdale and Buttermere, and Moore and I have also walked across to Grasmere and Rydal, we being the Wordsworthians of the party. We saw Dove Cottage where he wrote his good things as a young man, a small and old fashioned house with wood panelling, once looking onto Grasmere, the view now blocked by hotels. The rooms all very small, he living then in great poverty with his sister. The rooms which De Quincey* since added and inhabited also visible. A mile along the road – S.T.C.'s house, a one-storied white cottage, date 1702 on it, where he lived when Wordsworth lived at Dove Cottage. They used to walk together and plan *The Ancient Mariner* in those days. One would say there were men in England then, these people walking by the lakes with Sir Walter Scott to visit them, while along the hedgerows of the south Shelley is

*Thomas De Quincey (1785–1859); writer; author of *Confessions of an Opium Eater* (1821).

19

striding along at the head of his sisters, Byron lying on the Peachy stone, and Keats walking on Hampstead Heath. I got my schol. all right. Wedgwood was not given one, though he was classed by the examiners in the first class, this standing for his plays. I think it very hard that a man of Wedgwood's ability and industry should in his third year be denied a scholarship, which they give to men like Charlie Buxton,† people of very ordinary ability, in their *first* year. If it is not bolstering up classics, what is? However they have come to do their duty to history out and out, for there is a regular entrance scholarship for it now, besides giving me a major schol. in my second year.

Of course apart from comparison with Wedgwood I am very glad Charlie Buxton has got his schol. He and I will have plenty of money to go abroad this long now, wherever we like. Elliott has not got a schol., his unseens being so very bad, but is spoken of as certain next year. Buxton is a pull for Harrow training, – a 'point' for Moss. I had a very nice letter from Bowen. It ends – 'We have German measles here. 5 or 6 boys have gone home or are down with it, and some of the *very smallest* boys ask if the house is likely to break up'.

Please write me about the novel, if you write anyone about it, because I know about its plan and beginnings. I won't tell anyone if you do.

We are especially fond of scrambling in the upper part of the Derwent beyond Leathwaite, where it runs between high ridges of rocks and precipices. Wedgwood is a *really* good rock climber.

Your affectionate brother
G.M. Trevelyan.

I am going to see Moore's brother again in London next week. Write me to London not here, as I shall not be here long.

†Earl Sydney Charles Buxton (1853–1934); statesman; under-secretary for colonies,1892–95; president of Board of Trade,1910–14; Governor-General of South Africa, 1914–20.

And GMT's love for poetry had not diminished.

Trinity.

June 7.

Dear Bob,

When I was last in London I came across a manuscript poem – incomplete – on the fine and original subject of Epimetheus. Being myself engaged on a work yet unfinished, I felt a natural interest in and sympathy with a brother man engaged on producing literature or teaching himself to produce literature in this barren age when the giants are all seemingly dead and unborn.

Not knowing who he was, I still thought I would mention his poem to you, as you might know him.

I was really charmed with the story of the Gods and Titans in the first canto, which was not unworthy of so high a subject and had some of the divine afflatus in it. In the second canto indeed, the author seemed to me to lose command over the metre and style. But he is plainly a man who has a fine imagination and who can express it well in poetry, though not as yet for long together. If you meet him, encourage him from me to pursue the trade he has chosen. May Calliope sit with him at breakfast and Erato wander with him through the woods at mid-day. My mistress Clio, to those who know her best, is a great breeder of the imaginative and epic character of mind, although her loudest and most superficial acquaintances strenuously deny it. May my heart which is as warm as ever it was to the dead poet Shelley and his trade, ever be warm to the living poets and their trade, especially if they are in any sense my brothers.

Yr. affectionate brother

G.M. Trevelyan.

In the summer of 1895 GMT travelled to Switzerland. He kept a strict time-table, dividing his hours between sleeping, strolling and thinking.

> Hotel Todi,
> Thierfehd,
> Glarus,
> Switzerland.
> Summer 1895

Dear Bob,

Plainly the time has come for me to break the golden rule that you gave me last year when you were abroad, that the person at home writes first. Buxton has gone home, after we have visited many countries and cities of men together, and I have settled down in this remote valley cuddled up under the great mountain, for a fortnight's quiet work and thinking. I am having the most splendid time. *Perfect* health, which I have not had for the last year, though I have nothing to complain of in the way as things go, with our measly generation. I lead the true philosopher's life for a fortnight – triumph over matter in the shape of stomach, and complete independence of social intercourse, as they all speak German. The true philosopher rises at 5–30, runs out to bathe in the cataract, not forgetting his country and that Englishmen must wash. He has a big breakfast with eggs and chocolate at 7, works till he has digested his food, at philosophies of history (which will be the sole study of all philosophers in the future) then strolls out for an hour, revolving what he has read and gazes at the smoky back of the glacier. Then he comes in and works till lunch, which he takes at one o'clock – milk and bread and butter; if he were to dine with the glutton foreigner on three courses at midday, matter would triumph again. After lunch he goes out for his long walk and scramble on the hills and over the torrents, and returns at evening to write to his brother, and to read Homer or Vergil (in the original at last, such is his knowledge of the dead tongues). Then he dines with glutton foreigners, with *one* of whom he can converse in French – a fair lady whose heart he has won by presenting her with some golden lilies he has found on the high hills. The true philosopher ends the day by reading four chapters of the book of Job, which he has of late learned to admire, and at 9–30 he sleeps, till the sun, long-risen, calls him at 5–30. The odyssey and travelling have together made me realize the horror of distance. Without swift locomotion the feeling of distance from one's country would be unbearable. If instead of going by train, I knew I had to walk or drive by post-chaise and cross the sea in a doubtfully-sailing ship, my desire for my dear fatherland and the […] of the Wansbeck would drive me home at once. As it is, it is merely a pleasurable piece of sentiment. I often think the poem of the greatest horror remains to be written, describing the man who has got onto the moon by a projectile, and cannot get back. He sees his dear home looming by in the stage, but the horror and inevitability of space and distance holds him there.

I wonder if you are doing any novel at Wallington. It is very interesting to see what you will take to eventually. But I feel you, above all people, work out your own salvation and don't want advice. But I still hope you will take to 'one sided' history, that is telling the story of some great movement sympathetically, not critically or scientifically.

I am writing another Cambo Lecture, about England in the 14th century. It is great fun writing lectures for an uncritical audience after Cambridge. I expect to hear of C's election by telegraph tomorrow. If he gets in, he will have a wonderful start; I think his health is good enough now to allow of his success in life.

Write to me, my brother, for I am far away.

Yours fraternally,
G.M. Trevelyan.

Back in Cambridge GMT was a keen observer of some of his friends. And Robert ought to know what GMT thought of them.

Cambridge 1895
Nov. 2.

Dear Bob,

I hope you will be coming down here soon. I am very busy seeing people and getting to know them, and am finding plenty of friends of a younger generation, so I shall not feel shelved next year. It is particularly necessary to energize, as both Wedgwood and Moore are particularly lazy about getting to know people. Moore is so much more wrapped up in his metaphysics than he has ever been before, that it seems to make him quite unconscious of the outside world. He is getting worse and worse instead of better. He never says a word at Hall, or makes the least effort to get to know anyone. It is really rather sad, partly for himself, and partly because he might be so very valuable if he would make an effort to influence people or educate them. He is a King of debate, and we have grand meetings, largely owing to him.

There is a man of very great ability, Grey, our relation, whom I hope to see in the Society some time this year. He knows a great deal, and makes good use of his knowledge. He is a very powerful talker, with great intellectual energy and initiative.

Young Wedgwood is *very* young but very clever and original. He is a most charming fellow with an endless supply of spirits. If his brother is the Puritan he is the cavalier. I was at Locker Lampson's place the other day, seeing their library. The thing that interested me most was the Blakes. They had all his books in the original copies. He had them printed, the words that is and the outline of the pictures, and then painted in the picture with his own hand. The Songs of Innocence are most wonderful. The 'Tiger tiger burning bright' is grand. A tiger standing against a black background of night, *burning* with colour, red yellow and streaks of black. It is grand, and no one cares if it is not a tiger.

Uriel and the daughters of Albion are more Titanic. They are fearful and wonderful nightmares, some of the picture more 'dread' than anything I ever saw.

You should try and see these books, especially the Songs of Innocence in the B.M., where I think they are. They give one quite another idea of Blake's genius than even the Book of Job, where there is more thought and *possibly* less genius – tho' I don't like to say myself for I like Job best of all.

Your affectionate brother,
G.M. Trevelyan.

I have an interpretation for the Book of Thel which I should like to tell you about.

In the summer of 1896 GMT was off to Europe again, plunging, as he said, 'into the unknown for a fortnight'. In the rucksack he carried with him Shelley, Plato and the Hebrew poets.

June 1896
Hotel Zermatt.
Letters sent straight here now.

I am writing in a plainly furnished 3rd storey bedroom, with 'magic casements opening on' – the Matterhorn. In this noble garret, Plato, Shelley, Homer and the Prophets keep me company – nor let the inspiring, tho' not inspired, Baedeker be omitted. I shall be quiet here a week or so, till Buxton has to go, and then, shouldering my rucksack, plunge into the unknown for a fortnight. This is a nobler place than I ever had the wit to dream of, even in the night watches. I am preparing a letter.

★ ★ ★

Hotel Carron,
Fionnen,
Val de Bayne.
Summer 1896

Dear Bob,

I turn with joy from the task of answering a letter of Searle's, of which I could not read *half*, to the simpler task of answering yours. I am living here alone a week in this quietest and most beautiful of places, after a week of stirring adventure and sightseeing with Charlie Buxton. We mounted the Breithorn, and saw all the Kingdoms of the Alps in a moment of time, we descended into Italy by the Val Tournanches, by a path of violets which would have made your heart leap. We slept two nights at Aosta, where Roman walls, gates and triumphal arches are seen in the same *coup d'oeil* as the highest of the Alpine peaks! We crossed the Grt St Bernard (myself making heart-wearying Trevelyan jokes about Nap, which Buxton finally refused to laugh at). We slept at the hospice, bayed round by the hounds, and descended into Switzerland. Buxton has now left me and I have a week to think over it all, and in fact to digest the whole of this last year, which has been a year of great 'mercies' to me as they would have said in the 17th century, of 'development', as we say in the 19th. I am living on Shelley, Plato, and the Hebrew prophets. It is as impossible for a Hellenist poet like you to feel the Old Testament as it is for a Christian like Buxton. Their message is out of sympathy with both. As to Plato, the great thing I have got of the Republic is the idealization of mountain walking and climbing. I have discovered that I am taking exercise, not for the sake of the body, or to develop the muscles, but for my soul's sake, to 'develop my spirited side'. This is a great point gained, is it not?

I hope to see some poems when I meet you next. I wonder how the great Greek legend is getting along. Remember that it was a grand conception, the story itself.

Your affectionate brother
G.M. Trevelyan.

During the academic year 1896–97 GMT worked on his Fellowship Dissertation at Cambridge. At a meeting of the Trinity Historical Society in February 1897 he read a paper on his dissertation. Lord Acton, Regius Professor of Modern History since 1895, who was also present at the meeting was greatly impressed by GMT's presentation and encouraged the young historian to work further on his theme for publication. This GMT did, but he wasn't yet sure about his chances for a Fellowship.

P.S. I have just picked up Swinburne's *Life of Blake*, a book I have long been looking for. I think it is the place, far more than Gilchrist, where you can get at what Blake meant.

Trinity
Oct. 18, 1897.

Dear Bob,

Thanks for your letter. I'm afraid I was not the 'young person' who had taken out the Aeschylus. My classical education really stopped short of ability to reach the Greek tragic drama, tho' it includes Homer and to some extent Aristophanes. If there had been a rational system of teaching classics I might, with the same amount of work, have easily learnt to read the drama.

The Fellowships were given to very good men; the principle gone on was that of giving them only to men at their last chance, the electors very rightly judging that there were a lot of people so good that that principle alone was a fair one. At that rate Moore and Barnet★ are safe for next year, and I have other reason for thinking they are, from reports. That is very much as it should be, though it is a pity Moore could not be managed this year. *If* there *is* a third fellowship next year, I and several people run a chance. But the only thing that really matters as far as I am concerned is that my work was very much approved of, and seems to have surprised them pleasantly. So I can go on without discouragement or fear that I am not doing as good work as I hope.

I hope the various Greek young ladies, under your chisel, are becoming beautiful exceedingly and will soon, like Pygmalion's *come to life* in print. I am reading next Saturday.

Yrs. G.M.T.

★Lionel David Barnett (1871–1960); orientalist; classical tripos, Trin. Coll. Camb.,1894–6; professor of Sanskrit, University College, London,1906–1917; Lecturer in Sanskrit, School of Oriental Studies, London,1917–48.

GMT concentrated on his manuscript, which he wanted his father and brother (Robert) to read and criticise.

3, Hare Court,
Inner Temple.
6 P.M. Oct. 10, '98.

Dear Bob,

I came over here this evening to find you, but have missed. I am afraid I shall have to dine with Dons and people tomorrow night, so I shan't see you at 8 Gros. that evening, but I shall be up in town some time on Thursday or Friday and will make a point of seeing you if I possibly can. I shall not be able to go to Fatty's dinner, as I have such a great many things of exceptional importance to settle and may have to see people at any time. I shall be at Welcombe* Saturday and Sunday with Papa, talking to him about my dissertation, which must now become a book†. He is going to read it. I want you to read at least some of it as soon as you can and give me general opinions and criticisms. I cannot expect you to work at particular things, but I want general criticism, if you can spare time to read at least some big bit of it. I am not going to show it to any other *young* person, as I shall have such a lot of *elderly* academic advisers as it is, and too many cooks spoil the broth. Moore was quite certain, but I am a surprise.

I went and saw old Bowes (of McMillans, Cambridge) and he told me Jackson & Verrall had both bought M. & A. the day before, and that he was ordering a lot more copies for the window against the beginning of term. That nice person Mrs Jos. Wedgwood is very much pleased indeed with M. & A. Cambridge not having yet assembled I cannot tell you anything about the sale or of private or general opinions at Cambridge on M. & A.

Your affectionate brother,
G.M. Trevelyan.

*Another family home at Stratford.
†*England in the Age of Wycliffe* published in 1899.

The Longmans agreed to publish the book, which was to be: *England in the Age of Wycliffe*. The manuscript needed editing, and 'no one but a literary person would have been any use', although Robert offered to help but private circumstance prevented him from doing it. So GMT sought assistance from his Cambridge friend, A. W. Verrall,★ 'also my tutor – the most original exponent of classical and modern literature'

8 Grosvenor Crescent,
S.W.
Oct. 19, '98.

Dear Bob,

I am sorry to say my dissertation is in Longman's hands for a fortnight. It gives me, however, a free fortnight, so you shall have me instead of my book, if you can manage it. I have several engagements in Cambridge till the end of Sunday next. Can I come to see you and Roundhurst any time *next* week, viz. Oct. 24–29. Say what days would suit you best if you can have me for a night or two.

I will explain to you why it is Longman after all when I see you. It is, roughly speaking, on the principle that a bird in the hand is worth two in the bush. Papa has got him to do all he possibly can for me, whereas I might have found it difficult to become the 'most favoured nation' with any other firm, and should certainly lose time in the process of doing so.

Hoping to see you next week,

I remain
Your affectionate brother,
G. M. Trevelyan.

★ ★ ★

★Arthur Verrall (1815–1912), Fellow of Trin. Coll., Camb.; first King Edward VII professor of English literature at Cambridge, 1911. Works include: *Euripides the Rationalist* (1895).

Trinity College,
Cambridge.
Nov. 23, '98.

Dear Bob,

I hope we shall see you at Cambridge before the end of term. Dec. 9 is commem. and Dec. 10 the last Soccer meeting this term. We are quite likely to elect
Waterlow before the end of the term, so if you come up at all you will be extra
welcome. I have got Verrall to do what you kindly offered to do had not circumstances made it difficult. He has been through the first half of my book very
carefully and prevented a lot of bad things, and he is going to do the same for
the second part the next few days. I am extremely glad, for it wanted doing
badly, and no one but a literary person would have been any use. I shall be very
interested to hear what you have been doing since I was at Roundhurst, and
how the play is getting on. Come here if you can before the 10th. It is no use
after that.

Yr affectionate brother
G.M. Trevelyan.

If you want to come to commem. dinner nothing is easier.

And before the year 1898 was over GMT was already planning to travel abroad and relax.

> Wallington,
> Cambo,
> Northumberland.
> Dec. 31, '98.

Dear Bob,

Thanks for card. I am going for a few weeks to Egypt first, in February. When, leaving that, I 'come again to the land of lands' you will probably by that time be 'in a seaside place to the further south', where I will visit you for a while.

Ask Berenson★ if I may then come to him, viz. probably in the last part of March. I shall at any rate stay in Florence. I will communicate with you both before I leave England. Papa's book is coming out on the 11th of Jan. Mine will be early in the Easter publishing season.

I am profoundly interested by the coming struggle in France, which cannot be long delayed now. If the man gets out I shall burn a bonfire in my heart. May France live!

> Yrs fraternally,
> George.

★Bernard Berenson (1865–1959); American art critic and connoisseur of Italian art. Berenson settled 1900 in Settignano, near Florence; a brilliant conversationalist; his home, I Tatti, became a mecca for European & American intellectuals. Robert Trevelyan and Bernard Berenson were close friends; Robert often visited Berenson in Italy.

1899

On his visit to Sicily

GMT visited Sicily in February 1899. The places he visited he found 'exquisitely beautiful'. The prose is almost poetic.

> Hotel des Palmes
> Palermo
> Feb. 11, 1899

Dear Bob,

I am very happy here and have lots to see and do. I went up Monte Pelegrino
this morning and saw where I was, and saw also Aetna, as distinctive and unmis-
takeable as ever; so we have something in common to see together besides the
stars. I saw the Palace chapel by a bad afternoon light, but shall see it again by
morning light once at least, I was greatly delighted and interested by it. I am
going to Monte Reale★ tomorrow. I will meet you on the 19th evening, at the
Casa Polite, unless I hear to the contrary. I enjoyed the view of Mylae and
Tyndaris Bay immensely from the train; the carriage was empty and I could dash
about from one window to the other. It was a very good journey.

> G.M.T.

★ ★ ★

★Monreale!

Feb. 16, 1899

Dear Bob,

Today 'the subtle thief of youth hath stolen on his wing my three and twentieth year'. The sonnet was not in the *Golden Treasury*, but I knew it by heart. It ought to be in the *Golden Treasury*, and still more ought the sonnet to the nightingale, 'O nightingale that on your blooming spray', Milton's earliest poem and therefore his least puritanical one, perhaps the only poem of his in a purely poetical as opposed to religious mood and therefore as unique as it is good. I liked the Dutch picture at the top of the museum almost best of all things I have seen here, which is saying a great deal; it is exquisitely beautiful and I felt that pang at leaving off looking at it, which one feels only with very wonderful pictures, or pictures which one likes wonderfully. The Acteon metope was, I thought, the other very great thing in the museum. Segesta★ was so wonderful and beautiful that I will not say anything about it now. I do not expect Girgenti† to be so good, as it will not be so solitary. I shall probably reach Syracuse by the train that gets in at 9.43 p.m. on Sunday.

Yrs
G.M.T.

★Segesta, ancient city of N.W. Sicily.
†Girgenti (Agrigento), city in S. Sicily.

GMT publishes his first book.

When Longmans published GMT's first book *England in the Age of Wycliffe* in the spring of 1899, Henry Sidgwick*, the Cambridge philosopher, was one of its foremost readers. GMT was grateful for Sidgwick's evaluation.

> Wallington,
> Cambo
> Northumberland.
> Aug. 19, '99

Dear Sidgwick,

Your letter gave me very great encouragement, as well as pleasure. I am at present in a cold fit; I feel all the badness of my book as keenly now as I felt its few merits two months ago; I am genuinely uneasy as to the real value of second-rate history books and the justification for writing them. The fact that you have taken so much trouble to criticize my book and even to read its worst part of it twice, shows that you take it seriously, apart from what you say in approval of it.

I quite agree about the faulty construction of the first part, and the better way in which it should have been composed. If all the general description had come first, as you suggest, the story of the Peasant's Rising could have followed straight after the last paragraph of Chap. III, which leads up to it. This would have been an incidental advantage, over and above the other general advantage you point out. I am, I find, influenced a great deal by the opinion held of my book by some half dozen or more brothers of a certain age, for whose opinion I have most respect. For your expressed opinion I have perhaps most respect of all, because you are one of the few persons who never say what they don't think, and one of the still more select group who don't even force themselves to think what they wish to think.

The struggle across the Channel is now neither more nor less than God v. the Devil with the odds on the Devil. Military, Clericalism and Democracy together must beat mere brains. Certainly I shall never again call myself a Democrat, but a Liberal. I must say that now I am more sorry for the few brave

---

*Henry Sidgwick (1838–1900); philosopher; Knightsbridge Professor at Cambridge, 1883–1900; major work: *Methods of Ethics* (1874).

men who in every town in France are suffering social persecution and will soon suffer political proscription, than even for Dreyfus, for whom the bitterness of death must have passed, now that he knows his innocence to be known by every 'sane man in Europe. As to the religious side of it, I came across a stanza in Heine's Deutschland IV yesterday –

> 'Dummheit und Bosheit buhlten hier
> Gleich Hunden auf freier Gasse;
> Die Enkelbrut erkennt man noch heut
> An ihrem Glaubenshass.'

Yours fraternally,
G.M. Trevelyan.

P.S. Please remember me to Mrs Sidgwick. I hope to see you both quite well in October.

Cambridge gossip.

Sunday.
[No date]

Dear Bob,

I seize the first opportunity of decent quiet to write to you. I spent all yesterday in seeing people and getting my pictures and books in, with a view to being quiet today, as you know it is one of my fads never to be happy till my penates are erected. I have put your books in the gyp room. They were mostly school classics. I cannot say how very much I like the rooms; the two places I am fondest of in the world are the old court and the cloisters.

Amos is in Russell's rooms, Gooch in the rooms opposite Collins' rooms, and Dakyns in the tower by the carriage entrance. They are historical stairs, as Horace Walpole commemorates their steepness. A young friend of his lived up in Dakyns new rooms and so he went to see him, and describes how he went up, cursing at every step, and came down praying at every step.

MacT's* course of lectures are going to be attended by Amos, Gooch, a lady, and Dickinson† and Wedd probably. I have got a couple of statuettes of Assyrian kings – Sennacherib and Salamenassar, copied from the originals in the B.M. They seem to me very fine statues, and are almost as original ornaments as your Hindoo god was. I had no night in London on which to go to the play as I came by the late train. Amos is ill, having overworked himself, and so affected his heart. There is even fear of his being unable to work this year. MacT. says he is very far forward in his reading and might do his tripos with not very much more work if the worst came to the worst. Mrs Amos is down here, and I had tea with her and Maurice yesterday. Any founders day gossip or scandal? Write.

G.M.T.

The two fellows who live opposite you were here the other day, both in great force, Theodore bathing on a raw morning with Moore as usual. I'm afraid I forget your address.

*John M. Taggart (1866–1925); philosopher; lecturer in moral sciences, Trin. Coll. Camb.,1897–1923. Works include: *Studies in Hegelian Cosmology* (1901).
†G. Lowes Dickinson (1862–1932), humanist, historian and philosophical writer; Fellow of King's Coll., Cambridge.

Reflections after reading his brother's novel.

Wallington,
Cambo,
Northumberland.
[No date]

Dear Bob,

I have just read our dear brother's novel. It is not so bad as I expected. The commonplaceness of the story and the setting is so bold and unconventionally conventional that it does not of itself supply material for laughter. All about Harrow – that is half the book is to my mind good, that is true to life. He knows more of boys than I thought. His moralizations are these 'Boys are soulless barbarians, but in spite of this the public school is the most wonderful place and a great field for doing good to the commonplace barbarian. For the exceptional boy it is not suited, nor is it meant for him.'

Van and Searle appear, but no one else that I can detect. The most amusing part to me is the description of Harrow customs and details, which no one but an Harrovian could detect. The two figures are the young barbarian, and the swot, who make friends. The swot, the son of an evangelical household, is troubled with religious doubt, which is tracked through several chapters. This occupies the last half of the book. One has to read this part swiftly, but with respect as coming from a brother – one of the last of the *old style* of Xtian brethren, as I count Welldon. The morals to be drawn from this last or religious half of the book, are:

(i) religion may be false but it is necessary to happiness and conduct.
(ii) go to Trinity, not Balliol. The swot goes to Balliol, and finds people making epigrams instead of talking apostolically, and so, in an agony of religious doubt which finds no serious sympathy at Oxford, but only epigram to help it, he attempts suicide, becomes maudlin, and reverts to Xtianity. It is plain even Welldon considers his reversion to Xtianity rather a poor job, and forced on him, by necessity not reason. I should think the Balliol people will be very angry.

I am glad you are coming back before long. I believe Mama is asking Mc T. He certainly ought to see the Macaulay books, and Papa is anxious to show them him. He is not going to be asked before the time you propose to return.

I am getting very fond of the West Wood, especially the part round the China pond. I go there every morning for rest after my work, and inspiration of intellectual effort. There is great need for such a place at Cambridge. The backs are good, but too academical and not solitary or secluded enough. To get in among bushes and trees on a fine day is the real way to tear yourself from the world, and let your mind refresh itself by the action of fancy. I am beginning to find imagination of unreal company or circumstances very refreshing for a few minutes each day. I gather you have been accustomed to doing it from what you said once a few weeks ago.

The battle is going on lazily. An attack of the Hills corps on the road at Wall House has failed, though they have secured one of the three sides of the triangular cover (see map). At ten minutes before 8, the English guard corps begins to appear over Kip Hill, and Buonaparte being only just preparing to cross the lakes, it will be best for the Gonave Corps to gradually roll itself up down the road, to form a junction with him if possible, as they cannot hold their present position till Nap. comes. If you approve of this I will conduct the operation, which can be done keeping possession of the part of the road along which they pass, and can lead to no disaster. If it is possible to hold the *Wall Houses* till Napoleon comes I will make them do so. If not, they must fall back on East Wallhouse.

This seems to be the best plan, and I will conduct the operation unless you write to the contrary. If you would prefer to have the battle put off till you return, write to say so at once.

Yours fraternally,
G.M. Trevelyan.

See map over page.

Appreciating Robert's 'foolishness'.

Trinity College,
Cambridge.
Nov. 27, '99

Dear Bob,

I am glad you are a fool, for I believe in that folly very heartily. I am very glad there is only the due percentage of calculation in it and no more; but I am sure that the calculation, so far as it goes is good, judging from my strong recollection of a lamp-light evening with a lady of intellect and character apparently far above the average. The news is the first good thing of any real concern that I have heard for some time.

Your affectionate brother,
G.M. Trevelyan.

A walk in the countryside.

8, Grosvenor Crescent,
S.W.

Dear Bob,

Our letters must have crossed one another. It is very creditable to both to originate the writing. My letter was however so much the shortest and stupidest that I feel moved to send you another note.

Our stay at Lectoller came to an end on Thursday, the 11th, and I went up by myself for a couple of days to see the Tweed and Yarrow country. I got to Melrose on Thursday and saw the Abbey and walked on to Selkirk by the banks of the Tweed, seeing Abbotsford on the way. On Friday I started early and walked 20 miles up the Yarrow to a mountain loch called St Mary's water, and drove part of the way back to Melrose where I took train and back to London on Saturday, seeing Kelso Abbey on the way.

★ ★ ★

It is a most interesting county, and very beautiful. The famed Yarrow is a very fast stream about the size of the Wansbeck at sources, and also where it enters the Tweed it is about the size of the Wansbeck where it enters the sea, only it is deeper. I waded in above the knee – to get the feeling of how people were drowned in it. The Yarrow valley, unlike the Lake valleys, is very broad, with high pasture hills sloping, not coming down in crags into it, the sun consequently lighting it all up and dancing on the stream. The round hills and general aspect are a great relief to the eye after the craggy Lake District. There are a few farmhouses along it, and every four miles a great peel tower, of which Newalk castle is a most magnificent spectacle. These suggest plainer than words can tell what life in the Yarrow valley must have been like. The whole county is the epitome of Scotch history – you see four abbeys marked in my map. I saw two of them and might have seen all if I had stopped another day. They were *all* built by David I, between 1100 and 1150, when he married Henry's daughter and Normanized Scotland. He brought Scottish Kingship a society from Macbeth period of barbarism to the Mediaeval Scotland we generally think of, by introducing Norman Knights and barons (like the Bruces and Belliols) and by founding these abbeys and filling them with English monks. The 100 years of peace that followed were Scotland's great days. Then the wars with England began and lasted for 300 years, and here again the history is epitomized in the Tweed valley. Not another abbey is built, but the existing ones are largely destroyed, some to be rebuilt, like Melrose, some to remain as magnificent Norman ruins like Kelso. Enough, enough. I went to see the Moores at their home yesterday (Sunday). I enjoyed it enormously, saw *all* of them, and talked for three hours on end with Tom Moore, who certainly is the most delightful person. He is writing another great poem on a classical subject; I forget its name, but it is also some woman's. I'm going to Welcombe tomorrow for a couple of days before Cambridge. I'm awfully glad the book is getting on. I shall be most interested to see it when you come back. Your ode on me getting the schol. might be prefaced by describing how poetry and oratory (the Eng. Poem and the Trinity Declama) having thrust him out of their doors, he returned to the one girl who was always faithful to him and whom he will never again leave.

On liking sonnets.

Dear Bob,

I am awfully sorry you can't come. It causes great disappointment here, but we must have you next time you have a day off. I hope you will be about soon. I am stopping in with a cold too, caught skating on the Cam.

I like both the sonnet and the lyric, chiefly I think for the power in the metre. Sonnets are like blank verse in the art required for making them, which chiefly consists in fitting in the sentences and the lines together and making the proper breaks. I hope you will go on writing poetry. I think Pylades beautiful.

Your affectionate brother,
G.M. Trevelyan.

Life at Cambridge.

Dear Bob,

I am glad your experience as a lawyer will allow you to come down next Sunday, though I daresay it won't permit you to answer my letter. We are all very cheerful, and flourishing on our old lines, but we expect 'a sop', such as you, to be thrown us once a week. Of course you are only a 'sop' in our relations to Cambridge society. Russell and his brother have been this week's sops. I breakfasted and had a walk with Wedd this morning. It was the first time I had seen him really to talk to. He was quite all I had hoped or expected. I have given up the union altogether, and am not going to speak again. The resolution is an inexpressible relief to me.

Great revolutions have been effected this term. First: a lady was at MacT's 'Wednesday evening' last week. Second: an entrance list.

My exhibition has been started. This means a great deal. You see till now there have been only third year scholarships which attract no one to the college, so that the level of history at Trinity has been appallingly low. I imagine last year's Mays when everyone in both years got 3rds have induced the authorities to move in the matter; still more a gift of £2000 to the college from Lord Derby. Young bags has come up and is quite flourishing. Elliott is developing into the most delightful of fellows. I have found the kettle holder.

G.M.T.

P.S. The battle ended very quietly. A good many of the young guard were cut off in the retreat. I think you would have probably won the hill in time, but Villars would not have ventured it. My plan was good and succeeded in the main but was so badly executed that the result was very paltry. *Our Table* = Marsh, Amos, Wedgwood, V-Williams, Moore, Sankyns, Watkins, self, Buxton (my Harrow friend, 1st year).

1900

To Mrs Sidgwick, expressing his deep affection for the dying philosopher.

> Wallington,
> Cambo,
> Northumberland.
> Aug. 21, 1900.

Dear Mrs Sidgwick,

My father tells me he has heard from Arthur that all hope has been given up. If a fitting opportunity occurs, will you tell him that I bear him strong affection, that the memory of his friendship will be one of the stars of my life as long as it lasts, and the example of his mind and character a moulding influence upon my own, as upon many other worthier people.

If you do not find yourself able to give this message easily, I believe he knows it already, so do not trouble about it.

Do not on any account trouble yourself at this time by writing to me. I know you will appreciate my motives in thus writing (indeed I cannot help it), and I will take your silence for approval.

> I remain,
> Yours in the deepest sympathy,
> George M. Trevelyan.

About writing.

Trinity.
April 26, 1900.

Dear Bob,

Thanks awfully for your letter. It is I think a particularly fortunate find by way of music box. The McT's are delighted with their china. If you drop down here any day, *tant mieux*; if not I am too busy to get away to you before Holland at the wedding, though I may meet you by chance in London where I am coming up on various businesses on Monday and Tuesday next.

I took to heart a good deal you said to me last summer about writing, or at any rate I was helped by what you said to see the necessity of slow careful and thoughtful work at style. I don't say I have succeeded much, but at any rate I have tried and am trying, not in everything I do but in everything I do seriously, by which I mean the longer essays that I am writing. Tom Moore is coming here for Sunday. Come too if you can.

Your affectionate brother
G.M. Trevelyan.

On reading Wordsworth.

1900.

Dear Bob,

I am sending the books. We talk of nothing but the School board now. MacT is Rileyite of course, but Sanger and Dickinson are anti-Rileyite the former violently, the latter with such caution as you can conceive. I am going to the Old Boys' on Dec. 1. Are you going by any chance? What will there be to see in London about the 12th of December?

I must see all the sights of your classical city. In three days and three nights I must see all the sights. Are you going to be at Wallington for a few weeks or a few days this vac? I am reading Wordsworth, for the first time with any appreciation or enjoyment. What grows on one is that everything he says is *true*. That is, whether true or false in the absolute sense, it is at least the real thoughts of a man as they came naturally to him, not the imagination of a poet forcing his fancy into shapes. And considering this, the fertility of his thinking in the best poems is really marvellous. Matt. Arnold's selection is the only way I have yet found of getting at him through the mass of rubbish with which he surrounded his throne.

Your aff. brother,
G.M. Trevelyan.

On reading Ruskin.

Wallington,
Cambo,
Northumberland.
July 9, 1900.

Dear Bob,

The most inexpressibly stupid thing has been done, I fear by dear old Mrs Larkins who is an awful goose. I left instructions with her that the bureau was to go the day I left, a month ago, and sent the Railway Co. men to fetch it. But as the railway men wanted it packed and I hadn't instructed anyone to pack it, she has left it in my room all this time without telling me. However she says it is going today, and I shall write about it freely to the Railway Co. until I hear you have got it. When you do, send me my maps, which you had better keep as a hostage till then. I hope you had a fine time for your drive down to Grasmere if it came off. I am just reading the second vol. of *Stones of Venice* (as I always read Ruskin while I am writing to prevent falling into Macaulayese); I think as far as prose style goes it is his best. There are whole pages of his high-flying style, sustained and successful, such as he only attempts in little bits in most of his other writing. The proportion of bunkum is also smaller.

Love to Bessie; tell her I am really annoyed about the bureau because settling in to a house should be done as a whole and not in driblets.

Yours fraternally,
G.M. Trevelyan.

To his mother, on the character of a lady, whom a friend of GMT's intended to marry.

Trinity College,
Cambridge.

Dear Mama,

Sanger told me about it last night. I saw her, long ago, in Sicily, and remember that she is strikingly intellectual, and also very sensible and with a *look* of character, though of course I could not judge that in an evening. She has certainly been brought up severely well, a good background for an artistic sort of person. I am sure she knows what she is about, and will know.

I think it probable that it is quite an exceptional chance for the peculiarities required. How much he is in love with her I don't know, not having yet heard from him. I think it is all right.

Yours
G.M.T.

On his house master at Harrow.

Trinity College,
Cambridge.
May 16, 1900

Dear Bob,

I have written the article on 'Bowen in his House' that will appear in the next *Harrovian*. I hope you will think it right and not wrong when you see it; it was very very hard to do and I feel its inadequacy dreadfully; I only hope there is no impropriety too. There is of course no need to let it be generally known that it is mine, though I have no strong special reason for concealing it, since it is what I genuinely felt about him. It is unnecessary to say that the Editors were the first to move in the matter, and pressed me to write it. C. Colbeck wishes to know whether you and I 'would like dear Bowen's gun and bicycle', and asks me to let him know which would like which. He says – gun 'I can't speak for', bicycle 'new and good'. Will you please choose which you would like.

If you are going down to Harrow you can see him yourself and tell him. If not, write to him, and you might send me a line too. He will also want to know the address to which to send your choice. Give my love to Bessie.

Your affectionate brother,
George Trevelyan.

P.S. I shall be too busy to get down to you before going north, which I am doing rather early. I shall see you at Wallington no doubt.

Invites Bob to dinner in Cambridge.

Trinity College,
Cambridge.
Nov. 9, 1900.

Dear Bob,

The Jebbs★ have asked me to dinner at Sat. (17th) evening, and as I have refused them once before this term, I do not think I very well can again. Unless you go to the Verralls, you may like to have dinner in these rooms here, which are in a way common family rooms as the pictures proclaim, and ask whom you like to come. If you tell me who to ask – Moore or Dickinson for instance – I will ask him or them. Also as I say I am engaged for lunch on Sunday. You had better arrange for that *or* for dinner on Sat. with the Verralls.

I hope you will breakfast on Sunday with me here, and dine on Sunday if you like too. Any arrangements you want me to make for you, either to get you invited or to invite others, I will arrange when you write about them.

Yr. affectionate brother,
G.M. Trevelyan.

★Sir Richard Jebb (1841–1905), Regius professor of Greek, Cambridge, 1889–1905; helped to found Cambridge Philosophical Society; O.M. (1905).

On mutual relationship within the Trevelyan family.

> Wallington,
> Cambo,
> Northumberland.
> Aug. 27, 1900.

Dear Bob,

I was as much pleased with the kindness with which you told me about your own troubles this year, as with the way in which last summer you equally kindly talked to me about the way in which I might help to make the family life more cheerful. The two incidents together persuade me that I shall be understood if I write now to explain to you several things which you do not know, but which I am sure you will be very glad to know. I am writing to remove definite mis-understandings, and I hope you will therefore read my letter very carefully and give it more weight than you would if it was a mere expression of my opinion. It is a statement of facts.

In the first place you labour under a mistaken notion that there is a sort of tacit conspiracy of disapproval of you. I thought this was untrue, but I did not say anything to you when you were here on the subject, but waited until I had something definite to tell you. Now I have something definite, as both Mama and Charles have talked to me.

In the first place Charles began to talk to me about Elizabeth and you, saying that he thought you and she were getting happy and at home here. I ventured, rightly as I think, to tell him something of your relations to Papa, that is to say that Papa talked to you in the sense you described. I was not surprised to find that Charles was more disturbed by this intelligence than I was myself, – distinctly more vexed. He had all along, as I think Bessie saw if you did not, been doing his best to make you both happy and to get on good terms with you; all idea of the other sort of thing was completely shoved behind him, in the past when we are all 3 very disagreeable youths. I am glad, I say, that I told him this, as without it there was no touchstone by which I could gauge Charles' feeling about you, and give you assurance of a positive kind that *both* your brothers are your friends. (I hope therefore you will not be angry with me for doing so; I did it, not out of gossip, but for a definite object.)

The truth is, though you hardly realize it, that Charles is really quite as kind as I am, and at least as tolerant (perhaps even a little more so). I quite realize that

I have more subjects of conversation and of interest in common with you than he has and that he is not literary. But in the matter of approval of you and kindness to you and Elizabeth, there is no difference between him and me. We three have all chosen different lines of life, and have *very* differently constituted minds; there is no use blinking the fact. But we take each other as we find each other, and I see no reason why we should ever quarrel again. I assure you, you misunderstand Charles, at least as much as he does you. But at best this misunderstanding is not great, and I believe that the openness I have ventured to use as your common confidant will do something to remove it, and that his and your good feelings will do far more.

He is as loyal to you in conversation to me or to others, as I know that you are to him. If once you know this, I am sure no more difficulties will arise. In the second place, Mama began a conversation with me and asked me what I thought, telling me what had passed between you and her about Papa. She told me (what again I heard without surprise) that she had urged Papa in vain not to trench on the general subject of your life and work, and that she was really distressed that he did not take her advice. I told her what I thought. *She then asked me* (what I should never have ventured to do on my own account and had no thought of doing when you talked to me) *to speak to Papa myself.* Thus, so far from there being a kind of conspiracy of disapproval of you here, there is a kind of conspiracy to get Papa to forbear; there is also a kindness and an eagerness to do things for Elizabeth and you, which (on the part of Mama and Charles) ought not to be so obscure to you as it seemed to be when you were annoyed about the music. I am sure that if you had known they were fundamentally loyal to you, as I have now given you proof, you would not have been so aggravated about one matter alone.

As I say, Mama requested me to talk to Papa, and at her wish I did so. I must say with success. As this morning I talked in your favour to him, I will take the liberty of talking in his favour to you.

In the first place he was never proposing that you should give up poetry, or throwing any slight on it. He spoke again about article writing, because last year you had yourself told him you were going to, so that he had no reason to suppose it inconsistent with your other schemes. I confess this makes some difference, if you told him you were going to. To change your mind is of course legitimate, but you must see that it makes his talking about it far more reasonable, as being merely your own old idea of last year. Secondly he said he had no intention of continually recurring to the subject; in the conversation that arose out of the mention of Sidney Webb, he merely meant to suggest that you might interest yourself in some bye employment of education or politics, which many literary persons have found consistent with literary schemes as extensive as your own. He was not recurring to the main issue. However, the third thing he said is most important. He says he *has no intention of talking to you again about your work or general plan of life*, or of saying anything more to annoy you on the subject. That is as fair an offer as you could possibly ask for, and removes the last fear of any family difficulty that I can see.

The matter of expenditure, of keeping within yearly income, is quite another thing of course. We have all three of us adopted unremunerative professions, you and Charles absolutely, and I almost entirely. We are all dependent on Papa, as three sons very seldom are. Considering that he has not stood in the way of any wish or whim of any one of us, whatever he has *said*, but has always shelled out, we must put ourselves under his direction and meet his wishes as regards living within our incomes. It is the clearest justice to him, and a bargain which very few people could be fortunate enough to get out of their parents.

Furthermore, since we have all three chosen unremunerative professions, and since we are as a family burdened with landed estates, it is not merely a matter of pleasing Papa, but will be one of necessity, to undergo his direction in this matter. He treats you exactly as he treats Charles and me, in the matter of interfering to see that we do not run beyond our income. I think he is mainly in the right and ultimately wise in this question, even though he may use language that is exaggerated about the moral aspect.

You will see therefore that you need not be afraid of a continuance of that annoyance which you feared might diminish our family happiness here. If I seem to you to have taken liberties, they have been partly pressed upon me by Mama, partly encouraged by your own confidentialness with me, and partly undertaken by me because I thought the moment had come when a little plain speaking all round would clear the air for many a day. I have no wish to be perpetually talking on these matters. I should best like never to do so again. But please *now* read my letter carefully once for all, (and then burn it if you like). Answer only if you are inclined to. No need.

I am,
Your affectionate brother,
G.M.T.

On the possibility of arranging a meeting between Bob and George Meredith.

Wallington,
Cambo,
Northumberland.
Sep. 2, 1900

Dear Bob,

Your letter gave me the very greatest pleasure, and I cannot thank you too much for it.

I shall be down south in the middle of October, and shall come and see you then, or as soon as possible. It will be great fun!

As to the other poet who inhabits that neighbourhood, he said I might come and see him some time this autumn, and bring Theodore.* I promised Theo. to take him because he and I have often had talks about Meredith's poems and his view of life, so that there was a special point and pleasure in taking him. I also told Goldie about it, for the same reason. I can't do anything more *until* our visit, when I will certainly do what I find possible to do for you and for Mayer. I can't do more than that, but I shall be very glad to do that. In return don't tell any one else I know G.M., as I am anxious not to have it generally known by my friends. It leads to requests one cannot fulfil, but I shall do my best for you.

Love to Elizabeth, and tell her not to break all the dishes before I come in October.

Yr. affectionate brother,
G.M.T.

P.S. Tom has sent me his Altodorfer – and I have written for the Goya, about whom I have long been curious and unsatisfied in curiosity.

---

*Theodore Macaulay Trevelyan, GMT's son, died in 1911. His 'death was the greatest sorrow of my life' – GMT, *An Autobiography, op cit.* p. 29.

On the Boer War.

> Trinity College,
> Cambridge.
> Oct. 23. 1901.

Dear Elizabeth,

I am so very sorry to hear that Mr Hubrecht is very ill. It must be a great distress to you. I confess I am coming round to something much more like your Bob's view of the origin of the war, taught by the odious follies and horrors of the last 3 months. I was never a very strong Imperialist but now I am ashamed of having gone even as far as I did. Everyone I meet who is capable of thought and feeling is undergoing much the same change. But these are not a large proportion of mankind, and I do not see any near prospect of a reaction.

> Yours sincerely,
> George Trevelyan.

Letters to Robert Trevelyan

1901

On reading Bob's *Polyphemus*.

Wallington, Cambo,
Northumberland.
Dec. 23, 1901.

Dear Bob,

The book came out just after every one had gone down at Cambridge, but I will do all I can for it next term, the more readily as I like it so very much. I have ordered half a dozen copies to give as presents. I thought Roger's things were very romantic and beautiful and illustrated and explained or enlarged the idea of the poems a great deal, e.g. the swallow-mask and the bat. The vine-god and the Cyclops pictures were the others I liked best.

As to the poems I think *Polyphemus* is a great success, and better for the omissions. The ending as it is, is quite fine. The Propertius translation and the Apollo and Daphne translation were both very good, and together with the picture of Apollo and Daphne translated one into a world of romance and beauty. The 'Phasellus Ille' I cared less for.

The Beetle and Swallow Song I liked a good deal, but the Bat quite carried me away. I think it is much the best thing you have done, and in a way the most serious, in spite of its apparently trifling subject. It seemed to me quite an original vein of thought or fancy, most poetically worked out.

I hope you and Elizabeth are well and happy. I think if having brought out a good book helps to that, you should be. Lord Rosebery's speech is a funny business. After abusing the pro-Boers more strongly than anyone, he has said things that any pro-Boer would have been lynched for saying. I hope they will now get into common parlance. There is perhaps some chance of it.

As to myself, I went mad for two months last autumn, for reasons which it is unnecessary to explain, and saw men as idiots walking. While in that state I wrote an exceedingly mad article in a monthly magazine, in which a lot of truth was buried in a hopeless amount of bunkum. I am not anxious that you should see the article, but if you do don't judge me by it, for as I tell you I was temporarily mad, as most people are once in their lives. I am feeling better now.

Love to Elizabeth.

I remain,
Your affectionate brother,
G.M. Trevelyan.

1902

To Elizabeth, on reading Kruger's* and De Wet's† books.

> Wallington,
> Cambo,
> Northumberland.
> Christmas Day, 1902.

Dear Elizabeth,

It's a far cry to Ravello from here. The wild wind is loose, and the air is alive with noise and flying branches. Its idea of celebrating the birth of Christ is somewhat of the nature of pagan glee. It has knocked over one big beech already by way of celebrations. I hope you and Bob are having a sun-warmed and happy Christmas.

I am so sorry I have seen so little of you both lately, but this Review business is dragging me about all over the place so much just now; tell Bob we get the Prospectus out on Jan. 15. I will write him about it then if you are in Italy.

I have just read Kruger's and De Wet's books with the greatest interest. The old-fashionedness of Kruger, and his talk about 'the critical spirit coming from the Devil' is a curious contrast to De Wet's piety, which is much more in the background and relieved by a sense of humour and a habit of looking facts in the face.

A better, honester book than his, it is hard to imagine. He seems to be telling one all he really thinks both about friends and foes. And the things he says in indignation against the English are warrant of the genuineness of the fine things he says at the end in favour of loyalty to us. If he is too simple a man to be among history's greatest, he is certainly among the best of the great. Mama said to me something about Bob having the play published soon – Longmans'? I shall be very much interested if he is going to do so. The wheels of my book tarry rather with the Review and my Cambridge work, which latter I shall give up half of at the end of this year,

> Yours affectionately
> G.M. Trevelyan.

---

*Paul Kruger (1825–1904); South African Transvaal statesman; wrote *Memoirs*, 1902.
†C.R. De Wet (1854–1922); Boer general and statesman; his experiences in the South African war: *Three Years War* (1902).

1903

On GMT's engagement to Janet Ward★

Cadenabbica
20 May 1903.

Dear Elizabeth and Bob,
This morning I have got engaged to Janet Ward. Besides ourselves, everybody who is most nearly concerned, is very pleased, and when you know her, you will not be an exception to that rule. We shall not be married till next spring, and for a month or so now it is a secret, so please don't tell anyone.

But do ask Papa and Mama, and Charles more about it, and more about her; for I have unfortunately to be away the next 3 weeks. And it is so impossible to explain an entirely new chapter of things by correspondence. I can explain all when I see you. Hilton Young and Robin Mayor, my housemaster, also know about it, and dear Theo – and Booa. We are both very much in love with each other.

Your affectionate brother
George Trevelyan.

★Janet Ward, daughter of Mrs Mary Ward, neé Arnold (granddaughter of Thomas Arnold, 1795–1842, English scholar, headmaster of Rugby).

A request to review Thomas Moore's poems.

Address till Jan. 1.
Wallington.
Dec. 2, 1903.

Dear Bob,

The Committee hope you will write an article on Moore's★ poems (whichever ones you like) – roughly equal to 5000 words (or less) quotations being included in the calculation.

This, I gather, is not likely to be ready much before Easter. We hope it will be not much later at any rate. Good luck to you and Bessie if you're off to Italy.

Yours fraternally
George Trevelyan.

Of course if it had to come to 6000 I dare say it would do, but please aim at 5000.

P.S. Would you ask Bessie how we can describe Pierson on the cover of the review so as to show what a swell he is. Can we say *sometime Premier of Holland* – is that true, and is 'Premier of Holland' a proper title. By what can we call him besides his name and initials?

★Thomas Moore (1870–1944), English poet and critic.

A remembrance of the Mill House.

> Wallington,
> Cambo,
> Northumberland.
> Dec. 26, 1903.

Dear Bessie and Bob,
   Thank you very much for the postcard, which I shall always keep as a remembrance of the Mill House. I like mine, the back with Bessie in it, the rest a lot. It will be very exciting to see the other house rise.

> Yours affectionately,
> George Trevelyan.

1904

To Elizabeth, on her newborn son, Paul.

> Wallington,
> Cambo,
> Northumberland.

Dear Bessie,
   I must write and tell you what a dear Paul is. I did not see him when he was ill, and he is all brightness now. When I first went in to see him he thought for a moment I was his daddy and the disappointment caused a scene: but he soon got quite fond of me as I did not *touch* him too soon, which is the great secret. He is so like Bob, with his curls and all. We are great friends now.
   Don't answer this. Good luck to you.

> Yours ever
> George.

Disapproves of Desmond MacCarthy entering politics.

22 Sussex Villas,
W.
Jan. 30, 1904.

Dear Bob,

Thank you much for your letter. I am very glad you and Bessie have got such a jolly place. It is wet hell here.

I quite agree with you about Desmond; I disapprove of his taking up politics, at least I think I do, though Russell and Theo urge him on. At least if he could spend the time at

(a) reviewing for money and

(b) at writing reviews and books not for money, I think it would be better. His end in life is (b), but in order to do it and to keep his mother comfortable (much more ever to marry) he must also do (a). Why then if he is ill etc., does he complicate by doing (c) politics? I tell you what I think quite plainly, because if he goes out to you (as I shall try and get him to do) you might have some influence. He ought to distinguish between (a) and (b), which are 2 quite different things, and pursue *both* objects as hard as his health will permit – or he will go to the wall some day. He is very anxious, now, to make a little money to enable his mother to stop in London, and he certainly ought to do so. But he needs encouragement, as he never will begin to set about it by reviewing books that don't amuse him. He is not in a position to dictate the literary world and get the sort of reviewing he wants (as he is quite unknown) and therefore he ought not to pick and choose but do whatever he is given till he has got a place as a reviewer. Of course if he was well off I would not take this view, but would be very glad to see him do nothing but novels and high class reviews. But he and his mother are not well off. I enclose a letter of Tom's. Unfortunately we shall not be able to put in his article, I fear, and I am therefore extremely anxious to have your review of him this spring. He has stood so much from me in the matter of the Review, that I fear his honeymoon patience will be exhausted if I fail to get his poems reviewed, as well as rejecting his articles. Also I do greatly desire to get them appreciated at their true worth before the silly world.

Your affectionate brother
George.

Love to Bessie.

Admiration for Bob's writing.

Dear Bob,

I must write to say how very much I like your article and how warmly several people have spoken to me about it already. As to eulogy, it certainly if anything is too eulogistic, tho' not I believe too much so for the nature of the subject. But it is as high as eulogy can go without being fulsome.

Yrs ever,
George.

Fun in writing on Garibaldi.

Stocks Cottage,
Tring.
2 July 1904

Dear Bob,

Thank you very much for your very kind postcard. Of course I shall much want to hear your criticisms.

I am to do a *Causerie* for the Speaker on Benn, but not till the middle of June, as I did one on Hardy's *Dynasts* recently.

I am writing a book about Garibaldi in 1849, which is far and away the best fun I have ever had in writing; I had a splendid time walking over the ground at Easter. Did you ever read D'Annasyios?

Yrs ever,
George.

1905

On reading Bob's *Parsival*.

> 2, Cheyne Gardens.,
> S.W.
> Feb. 15, 1905.

Dear Bob,

Thank you very much for *Parsival*. I think it a great success, and so does Jan, and so do the Frys, whom I met just now. We all find it as poetical as anything you have done, and as highly perfected in technique, but we also agree in being interested and moved by the subject and the idea, more than in anything you have done before. I think it is almost immeasurably better than Gonzaga, tho' I can quite see how Gonzaga taught you to write it. I find the central idea – Prometheor defiance of God – very gravely and finely worked out, and the dramatic and story telling part quite exciting or at least very interesting. I certainly read it with much greater pleasure than I read 9 poetical plays out of 10.

The best poetical thing is about sleep, 'Indolent waves breaking over and over' – that's jolly good – worthy to stand among great passages of poetry, and the dream is very good. Whether you have succeeded because it's a drama or in spite of its being a drama, I am unable to tell.

Thank you for it very much. Nothing has happened here yet. Love to Bessie.

> Yours ever,
> George Trevelyan.

The first part of the first Act, up to the moment of his going mad is the least good – that was what you read me at Westcote, when I did not evince as much enthusiasm as I feel for the whole play.

Thanking Bob for reading the proofs (*Garibaldi*).

Stocks,
Tring.

Dear Bob,

Many thanks for your work at the proofs. It will make a great difference. It will quite do if you send the rest as you suggest.

The rhetorical passages in this batch are very clear cases for omission.

Love to Bessie,

Yrs ever,
George Trevelyan.

1906

On the salaries of civil servants.

2, Cheyne Gardens,
S.W.
Dec. 10, 1906.

Dear Bob,

I have signed the transfer and sent it on to Maurice Bell. I saw Hawtrey about the B.M. salaries question. It appears that the scale of pay is the same as for the majority of the Civil Servants, though the Treasury, Home Office, Education and India, and I think one other, are higher. I think they ought to be on the higher scale, but I fear the Treasury would be stiff. Charles says he will enquire as to the pay of the higher posts in the B.M., whether they offer less or more than the posts the ordinary Civil Servant rises to. He is inclined to ask about it and find out more. Whenever you see him prod him about it. He is quite sympathetic and inclined to do anything if anything can be done.

We are waiting for news about Bessie. It is troublesome this waiting.

Give my love to her and to Mama.

I leave England on Friday morning.

Your affectionate brother
George.

1907

On writing an Introduction to a book on history.

Mantua.
April 13, 1907.

Dear Bob,

Many thanks for your letter, which has pleased me very much. The printer seems to have run short of 'f's, after the final proof stage. I was annoyed about 'our' cannon in particular, as it made wrong sense which is worse than nonsense. But a patriotic romance can be founded on the error: as thus: young Bonaparte, really out to conquer the world, swears to send the first English cannon which he captures to the Sanmarinesi, he spends the rest of his life, year by year, till the Gods are tired, *trying to capture an English field piece for the Sanmarinesi*, in Spain and elsewhere, and *never does* – let us say.

I agree about the Introduction. If one could assume one's audience as for a work of literature, it certainly ought to have come later, if not at the end. But in the present state of history in England, a history book is treated as an historical monograph, and consigned to historical students, unless it violently proclaims that it regards itself also as literature and appeals to the general public. My introduction is intended to set out the nature of the book and of the theme, and while what you say is *quite true*, it does not absolutely follow that my plan was wrong, people being what they are nowadays.

I am glad you see a nearer approach to chastity in the style. I do not claim to have achieved chastity altogether, but the nearer approach is something, and it is largely due to your very kind and painstaking efforts over the 'Stuarts', for which I shall always be most grateful. You really taught me not a little.

We are having a splendid time in Italy; I am glad to hear Booa is better; I fear she was really bad. My best love to Bessie and to Paul, in whom having not seen, I yet believe.

Your affectionate brother,
George.

A private note.

2, Cheyne Gardens,
S.W.
Oct. 7, 1907.

Dear Bob,

I am very sorry about the news contained in Withers' letter, which I suppose you have by this time received. I am very sorry her personal property is so small. It doesn't much matter about Hallington, one way or the other, whatever happens. Janet wants to know whether Mrs Sturge Moore has recently had or is about to have another baby; – because if not we were going to ask them to dinner. Would you ask Bessie to send her a line about it, at once, as I expect you know.

Your affectionate brother
G.M. Trevelyan.

1908

On reading Bob's *Sisyphus*.

2, Cheyne Gardens,
S.W.
Dec. 2, 1908.

Dear Bob and Bessie,

I have just got *Sisyphus*, which looks very well. Very many thanks for it. I shall read it again with great pleasure. I like it the best, for it contains more of 'Bob' in it than his other works. And I have a natural liking for the grandiose and grotesque in literature.

I will see if I can arrange about the Tramps coming down some Sunday that will suit you early next year. I cannot arrange it for this Sunday, as I cannot see Stephen and he is a person there is no use writing to as he does not answer letters. And it will want some planning, as we shall have to see what trains back we can catch etc.

Yrs ever
George.

P.S. I don't mean Bob is grotesque!!

GMT informs about the birth of his son.

2, Cheyne Gardens,
S.W.
11 p.m. July 5.

Dear Bessie,

You will be delighted to hear that we have got a son and that Jan is doing very well. It happened half an hour ago.

Tell Bob, whose address I do not know.

Yours ever,
George Trevelyan.

On reading Bob's *Don Quixote*.

2, Cheyne Gardens,
S.W.

Dear Bob and Bessie,

We have for some time been reading nightly out of your *Don Quixote*, with great enjoyment, and today the most beautiful lot of Tourgenieffs in a delightful binding turned up. They are very nice indeed and look splendid in the long shelf with the other sets of novels. I am going to take one away next month. They give us very great pleasure.

Yours ever,
George Trevelyan.

I have been hearing from Desmond what a jolly time you have had.

1909

Thanking Bob for his editorial help.

Tyn-y-Fron,
Betwys-y-Coed.
Oct. 1, 1909.

Dear Bob and Bessie,

Bessie will read this and send it on to Bob at Settignano. We are staying a day or two with an Aunt of Jan's here, and returning to the neighbourhood of London (Stocks) in a day or two. We shall be in London again on Oct. 9. I am lecturing at Bradford on this day week and staying there with the Herbert Joneses to whom I will remember you. I will certainly manage to see Bessie this next month or two, and much looking forward to doing so.

It was very good of Bob to read my book before writing to thank for it. It is such a bore to get letters of the 'I will lose no time in reading your book' order.

I was immensely gratified by Bob's approval which was more complete than I had expected – probably more complete than I deserved, for I see *The Times* [in what may otherwise be regarded as a blast of trumpets in favour of the book] still finds my style unchaste in places. But at any rate it would be much worse but for Bob's 'taking me in hand' over the Stuarts. There are so few *critics*, and none of them appear in print at least not over history books, which escape all *literary* criticism. Raleigh's *Wordsworth* seems to me a very fine book. I have just read it with immense delight. I find myself becoming more and more a Wordsworthian.

Best love to you both.
Yours fraternally
George.

Jan sends her best love.

Yes – I said *all I knew* about Cavour's and the King's thoughts, which is very little because Cavour contradicts himself (viz. lies) in his letters and the King's papers have never been published.

A note to Bessie.

Nov. 17, 1909.

Dear Bessie,

I think this is a really dear old letter, and I am human enough to prefer such 'thinking aloud' to 'propriety', though I daresay I shouldn't have written it myself. Still, I hope I shall be spared a correspondence for my own part!

I am extremely pleased that you like my book so much, for I value your opinion highly – and it always means something real. You are quite right about the Sicilians. But for my debt to individual Sicilians, which is really considerable, I could have been more humorous at the expense of their absurd countrymen. What a jolly time we have on the Fifth of November! I am lunching with the Jans at Cambridge tomorrow.

Yrs ever

George.

I know about Aunt Annie and have heard from her.

1910

In Italy.

Bologna,
Feb. 6, 1910.
Address – 2 Cheyne Gardens,
London, S.W.
To be forwarded.

Dear Bob and Bessie,
This is just to say that I am thinking a great deal about you and waiting to hear good news. I shall be in Rome in a few days now, which I always like. It is curious but once I am in Italy I feel a kind of dissatisfaction till I am in Rome, however much I am enjoying myself elsewhere. I believe very few other people feel it.

I shall have to live in Naples a fortnight some time in March, which will be an effort, but fortunately one of the Huxley youths★, a grandson of *the* Huxley and a cousin of Jan's, is working at the great biological marine station there, and I shall be able to live with him. He is a clever fellow and very nice and a good liberal I am glad to say. It is curious how much one cares about that nowadays.

Janet will let me know. Don't bother to telegraph or write for I am most anxious to spare you trouble and I shall hear as soon from her.

Your brother
George.

★Sir Julian Huxley (1887–1975); zoologist and philosopher; first director-general, UNESCO, 1946–8. Works include: *Evolution, the Modern Synthesis*, 1942.

On reading Rhoda Fleming and meeting a Balliol philosopher.

Grand Hotel Trinacria
Palermo.
March 1, 1910.

Dear Bob,

I hear that your baby was ill under circumstances which naturally caused great anxiety. Fortunately for myself I got a telegram to say it had recovered before I got any letter on the subject. I am very sorry that Bessie should have been put to such a strain, and it must have been a very bad time for you. I hope all is well now.

I arrived here last night. I like this place as much as I hate Naples. Everything about it charms me and rests me, even on a bad day like today is.

I am reading Rhoda Fleming again and this time thoroughly agree with you about its inferiority. I remember you saying it was 'melodramatic' and quite beneath him. I now entirely agree. It is as if the alleged 'illegitimate-son-of-the-Lytton' element in him, which is always visible and adds a necessary spice to most of his works, had here got complete hold of his mind for the time. *Except Rhoda and Dahlia*, the characters are all made to order on other conventional expectation; that is a much more serious defect than the mere melodramaticness of the story itself. Mrs Lovell, the wicked worldly widow, is such a miserably inferior edition of the Countess de Saldar in *Evan Harrington*, who is at least created by G.M.'s imagination.

As to politics it is no use writing or even talking about them. I hope God will inspire our leaders to retrieve the situation that some insane devil has induced them to throw away. We must all be loyal, so the less said the better.

I can imagine Bertie talking on the subject of Sir E. Grey*!! I met a very nice Oxford, Balliol Don at Naples, called Smith (not A.L. but J.A.† I think). He was a philosopher by profession, and I thought a very good one, and a very good man. He had a great contempt for the pragmatists and Christians and great admiration for Bertie, and discussed Henry Sidgwick and McTaggart excellently and critically. He was an excellent Liberal too. He seemed to me a splendid person to have teaching the cleverest young men in Oxford in their Greats course. In a way he was much better suited to be a teacher of youth than

---

*Sir Edward Grey (1862–1933); statesman; foreign secretary, 1905–1916; Chancellor of Oxford University, 1928–1933.
†John Alexander Smith (1863–1939); philosopher & classical scholar; Waynflete Professor of Metaphysical Philosophy at Oxford, 1910–36.

more brilliant men. I expect there are good things about Oxford. At Cambridge
there are a few great philosophers. At Oxford the young men are taught little
philosophy. It is perhaps not a bad division of labours.
Yours ever,
George.

Don't bother to answer, but give my very dearest love to Bessie and to the boy.

On the Academic Committee of the Royal Society of Literature.

Stocks Cottage,
Tring.
May 24, 1910.
Dear Bob,
Thank you for the £3. 13. 6 which I have sent on with a similar cheque of
my own. I hope we shall buy a nice acre, lots of bracken and birches and part
of a beck. I agree with your fears that it may stimulate the landlords to black-
mail us, but there are dangers in every policy. So far the Society has only bought
or attempted to buy land already threatened to be made building land, and which
certainly would soon have been covered with villas but for their action.
By the way, the proposed Academic Committee of the Royal Society of
Literature, which I told you about, seems likely to be a harmless, if useless and
unimportant body. All its members that I have talked to view the idea of its being
an 'Academy' or 'crowning' books etc., with as much horror as I do. Its object is
to prevent the fatuous dons who compose the so called 'British Academy' from
posing as the official representatives of Literature, as they did on the occasion at
the Tennyson Centenary and Meredith's* death. The proposed estate objects of
the Academic Committee – which I objected to – are the words of the Charter
of 1824 incorporating the Royal Society of Literature, which since that year has
done nothing to carry out those 'objects', and now proposes to form us as a Committee to not-carry-out the objects in its place. At present it is private, so don't
talk about it. I am happy to think it will never be much talked of.
Yrs ever.
G.M.T.

★George Meredith (1828–1909); novelist and poet. GMT wrote *The Poetry and Philosophy of George
Meredith* (1906).

1911

A private motive.

2, Cheyne Gardens,
S.W.
Jan. 23, 1911.

Dear Bob,

I agree with all you say in your letter about the story. If I was put in the box I would give evidence in the strongest possible way for Tom's character and motives; and I could give my firm conviction that the story is neither immoral in tendency, nor indecent (in the only sense I know of the word, viz. as exciting or meant to excite lust). I have written to Tom that I will do anything that could help if his character or happiness is involved. Otherwise I am of course extremely anxious to keep out of it. It is not the sort of controversy I care much about from the *public* aspect of the quarrel, but from the private point of view I will do anything necessary if I am asked.

If Tom asked me only because I was an academician, I am *not* an academician. I hope we may hear no more about it.

Yrs ever
G.M.T.

Appreciates Bob's approval of GMT's
Garibaldi and the Making of Italy **(1911).**

2 Cheyne Gardens,
S.W.

Dear Bob and Bessie,

Thank you both very much for your letters. *(As* I am not certain of Bob's address I am writing *one* letter to be forwarded on.)

I am very glad you both liked *Garibaldi III*; I very much appreciate your approval of it because you have critical standards. I am much obliged for the corrections.

We saw Will A.F★ as he passed through London on his belated way out to Italy. He suffers badly from the A.T. (Artistic Temperament) about arrangement, saying what *he* is going to do, keeping appointments etc. His big Malvern picture and portrait of Janet were *finished* the day before he sailed, and they have both gone to the Newbury Art Show – if accepted.

I am very glad Bob is with the Abercrombies. These Tripoli horrors and the whole folly of the war discourage me terribly. I don't think I shall have the heart to go to Italy again for many years. I have got to bring out in a week or two the 'English Songs of Italian Freedom' of which Bob read the Preface, but I have no heart for it now, or even for Garibaldi.

I am delighted to hear about the Stadtholder's earliest remarks. It is good to think of him.

Yours ever,
George.

Love to Papa. I shall see Mama tomorrow.

★Arnold Forster Will, the artist, Mrs Ward's cousin.

Expressing sorrow at Bob's having lost his child, Paul.

Robin Ghyll,
Langdale,
Ambleside.
Apr 24, 1911.

Dear Bob,

Thank you very much indeed for your letter, and for going to Swanage. I am sorry it was in vain. I did not write or wire to you because I knew you had left the reading party for Will's, but none of us knew where that was as I could not communicate.

This is a very great blow indeed to us, but it can scarcely be as great a blow as that which reduced you two from the state of having offspring to the state of having none at all.

Your courage then is an example to us now.

Your affectionate brother
George.

★ ★ ★

Aldbury
Oct 4, 1911

Many thanks for your p.c. I noticed and liked the sonnet in looking through Rossetti★, and felt and feel uncertain whether to put it in or not.

The action of the degenerate Italians of today in going to conquer another race at the expense of European peace takes the heart out of me as far as my books are concerned. I hope you will have a good time in Tuscany.

Yrs ever
George.

To. R.C. Trevelyan Esq.,
The Shiffolds,
Holmbury St. Mary,
nr. Dorking.

★Dante Gabriel Rossetti (1828–1882); poet and painter.

1912

On reading Bob's *The Bride of Dionysus.*

2, Cheyne Gardens,
S.W.
May 1, 1912.

Dear Bob,
Thank you very much indeed for *The Bride of Dionysus.* I have read it with the greatest delight. I think it is much the strongest thing you have published, with the possible exception of *Sisyphus,* and that was so different. I like the short poems and the Lucretius and Attys very much too. *The Bride* is the only good libretto I have ever read. It is poetry and drama and yet very much of a libretto. It does not go to pieces anywhere. Theseus is really fine and says fine things. The incantation by Phaedra is very good poetically and I should think ought to be so operatically. Your conception of Dionysus is I think right, certainly legitimate and successful. Will A.F. tells me you and Vernon Lee★ had a royal row over it; so far as I understand the question you are quite in your rights to have someone more dignified and fundamental than Titian's 'Bacchus', who is after all called 'Bacchus' of the cinquecento, not 'Dionysus' of modern archaeology.
I greatly hope you will be able to have the opera done.

Yrs ever,
George.

Love to Bessie and Julian.

★Vernon Lee (pseudonym), Violet Paget (1856–1935); author; works include: *Studies of the Eighteenth Century in Italy,* 1880; *Renaissance Fancies and Studies,* 1895.

Letters to Robert Trevelyan

1.

Wallington,
Cambo,
Morpeth.
Sep. 12, 1912

Dear Bob,
  It is very interesting that you are going to India and I hope both you and Goldie will enjoy it and get all you hope for out of it. If Bessie comes here in last days of Sept. I shall be here or at Cambo, though not Janet.

Yours ever,
George.

Don't bother to answer.

2.

2, Cheyne Gardens,
S.W.
Oct. 11, 1912.

Dear Bessie,
  I have arranged with Rothenstein★ that I am to go up to him to be sketched some time early next year. I am too busy before Xmas. I have told them to send a copy of the Meredith poems coming out next week, to you at the Shiffolds. Papa and Mama will get a copy at Wallington, so you can either leave it at the Shiffolds or send for it as you like. The *letters*, out this week, are well worth reading.

Yrs ever
G.M.T.

Love to the Stadtholder. No answer.

★Sir William Rothenstein (1872–1945); painter; principal of Royal College of Art,1920–35.

1913

On Tagore and Yeats

2, Cheyne Gardens,
S.W.
March 7, 1913.

Dear Bob,

I have sent your letter on to Swan. I am very glad you are coming back to the Lake Hunt. I have been hearing a lot about India from various persons, white and brown, and have become quite a Tagorite★, under the teaching of Yeats†, W. Rothenstein and one of T's pupils called Ghose. Tagore has stopped Yeats being mad on magic and small green elephants, and has cleared his mind of much superstition, I am glad to say. And when clear of an impossible quantity of his magic nonsense, Yeats is one of the really splendid people. The excitement in Europe, apart from the Balkan war which bids fair to end very well, is to see whether Goldie will like his Chinaman as little as the Webbs‡ when he meets (and smells) them. From the address Bessie gives me I judge that you will be on the spot at this great meeting. I hope Goldie will not be like Matt Arnold, of whom H. Sidgwick said that he was like a dog, he judged everything by its smell.

I am glad you have had some good bathes, but don't be eaten of crocodiles. If you suffered the fate of Capt. Hook Mary could never read *Peter Pan* again and that would destroy her faith in life, or at least in literature.

I have just finished writing *J. Bright*§ and hope to publish in May or June.

Yrs ever
George T.

★Sir Rabindranath Tagore (1861–1941); Indian lyrical poet; Nobel Prize for literature, 1913.
†William Butler Yeats (1865–1939); Irish poet and playwright; Nobel Prize for literature, 1923.
‡Sydney Webb (1859–1947); wife, Beatrice Webb (1858-1943); both leading social reformers.
§*The Life of John Bright* (1913).

Appreciating Bob's approval of GMT's *Bright*.

Robin Ghyll,
Langdale,
Ambleside.
July 13, 1913.

Dear Bob,

Thank you very much for your letter. I am extremely glad you like the *Bright*, and what you say shows that you understand both the difficulties and possibilities of the task. You are also quite right that one never gets quite inside Garibaldi: I don't think he was ever quite inside himself!

Janet is getting steadily better. We have a masseuse for her back, but in a week we hope she will be quite all right again. She injured a muscle jumping over a flower-bed. Tell Bessie to be sure that she does not do that!

I much appreciate Bottomley's★ approval of *Bright*. I will send along some very lengthy and not very easily legible letters of mine about my travels, in a few days, as Bessie says she wants them. At this moment I am composing articles for the *Nation* and *Contemporary Review* out of them.

Yrs ever,
George

★Horatio William Bottomley (1860–1933); journalist and financier; Liberal MP, 1906–12.

On the situation in the Balkans.

I enclose a *Contemporary Review* article of mine.

Robin Ghyll,
Langdale,
Ambleside.
July 30, 1913

Dear Bob,

Thank you very much for your letter. I quite agree with what you say about the present situation, but I am terribly anxious for fear that the Greeks and Serbians will behave foolishly and brutally, and make the Turkish difficulty a very great one. Venizelos* is sensible but his Greeks are maddened by the idea at leaving their 'brothers' in Thrace under Bulgarian rule. The fundamental difficulty is that the ethnography and geography don't answer to one another.

I wrote to Herbert and got the enclosed reply. It amounts to nothing. His information was, apparently, about Prizrend not Komanovo. At Prizrend there was only one Serbian division, and the whole affair was hardly more than a big skirmish. I daresay there were no Turks there; the Serbians themselves always spoke of it as a battle against Albanians. I do not think this is a case for me to try a 'contemporary history'. After all good contemp. histories like Thucydides, Clarendon and even Burnet were written by men who lived in the affair and were natives. I know nothing about the Balkans and know no Balkan language. And the Balkan peoples *all* lie like the Devil.

Love to Bessie and Julian,

Yrs ever George.

Janet is well again now.

---

*Eleutherios Venizelos (1864–1936), Greek statesman; Prime Minister of Greece, 1910–15, 1917–20, 1924, 1928–32, 1933.

1914

On the approaching war.

> Wallington,
> Cambo,
> Morpeth.

Dear Bob,

Thank you for your very kind letter which did my heart good. I am afraid I take a more serious view of England's positive *danger* than Charles (and perhaps than you) and am going to go further than you may like in the way of arguing the greater justice of our cause than Germany's to the Americans, whose friendship is so essential.

You will not agree with all I may say or do, but that you should so generously recognize that I am acting to the best of my conscience and not from funk is a great thing to me.

> Yours ever
> George

Robert Trevelyan to GMT on the outbreak of the war.

26 Aug. 1914.

My dear George,

As I have reason to believe that in some degree at least, you are not quite in sympathy with the views which many of our friends hold upon present events I thought there could be no harm (and I hope you will think so too) in my putting down and sending to you what seems to me the main reasons for taking a strong line against the Cabinet, both as to its past action and its present action, and I fear, its future action too. Since I began, I have just had a long and I fear sometimes heated argument with Amos, than whom personally no one could be nicer, nor more good-tempered, but whose whole vision and perspective seems to me to be distorted, as almost everyone's seems to me. It made me realize the tremendous gulf between those who think as I do, and others. The essence of the difference seems to me that some of us see clearly now that war between civilized people is absolute insanity, and nothing else, just as much as sacrificing children to Moloch was. (As to the Balkans that may be another matter. There probably people like fighting and have far less to lose.) The Carlyle passage in Sartor, you know what I mean, is the only way of looking at it, when once one sees it that way. Well, people like Amos, that is nearly all the nice intelligent reasonably peaceable, anything but brutal people, don't realize this. If they did, their whole vision would be changed magically, and they would see the whole foreign politics, diplomacy, honour of the nation etc. game for what it is, that is the most colossal system of humbug, wickedness that could possibly be imagined; in fact so colossal, that mankind has only arrived at it by blindly drifting, thinking almost entirely of other things all the time, so that the expert players at this fascinating game of creating inevitable wars have gone on unwatched and unsuspected. Everything, diplomacy, treaties, national honour, armaments and the rest seems to them a necessity, more or less deplorable, but at the same time the most natural thing in the world, whereas it is really the most unnatural and unnecessary. Now there are a few people whose eyes are open, and you know how they see things, whether they express themselves with passion like Russell, or more calmly like Charles★.

Now how, looking at it all with open eyes, does it seem to me. First Belgium,

★Both Bertrand Russell and GMT's brother, Charles, were outspoken pacifists, against Britain joining the War.

the stumbling block to so many good people, including Papa. Well first it is clear, whatever the fault of Germany be, that we are directly responsible for the destruction of Belgium. Our Cabinet, playing its selfish game of making war on Germany to the best advantage to itself, has encouraged the Belgians in the attempt to keep the Germans out, which of course they had no chance of doing, promising them support, which could not possibly reach them till their country was destroyed and all this merely to gain a strategic advantage to ourselves and our friends. If our concern for Belgium had been real, we should as Charles says, have advised them to let the Germans through under protest, and promised to do our utmost to get the Germans to keep their offer of respecting Belgian independence when the war was over, even to the length of fighting Germany, if it violated their independence. That was the only honourable course for us to take. (This is even leaving 123 out of the question.) As to Germany, as I read the situation, she considers herself fighting for her life against Russia, and therefore against France too, and that being so, thinks it may take any advantage, legitimate or no. That may not be the right attitude, but it is a perfectly possible one to understand. We at least, who bombarded Copenhagen, should understand it. Besides, I expect the Germans were right that the French would have tried to invade through Belgium (if they had had time) which we of course would not have prevented. Be that as it may, however brutal one may think German methods of invasion are, (I wonder what Russian methods will be, or Italian and Serbian methods were) I cannot think that any intelligent person can seriously suppose we had any right to go to war for the sake of Belgium. In fact, of course, we did not. It was merely taken hold of at the last moment to make this unrighteous war of diplomatic national hatred into a 'righteous' war for a small oppressed people. The real causes of war are elsewhere. Now after talking with a number of intelligent people, Amos, Berenson, and others, and reading the less offensive things in the papers, I really can find no fundamental cause, except a vague indefinable suspicion and (though it is not usually admitted) dislike and even hatred of Germany and Germans. No one is really able to say what it is the Germans were going to do against us or against the French. They obviously could not invade us, nor except to a lunatic, could it seem possible that they could want to. They had nothing to gain by crushing France again, as they know by experience that annexation is a mistake. There was Morocco, it is true, and there were doubtless many other possible Moroccos, of more or less importance, but none of them worth going to war about, even from the worldly point of view. No, the whole enmity and suspicion was unreasonable on both sides, and in our case it was far more unreasonable and wrong than in that of the French. We were free, till we bound ourselves. The French thought, wrongly I think, that they must bind themselves to Russia, and then I grant, after that folly, they had some reason to be afraid. And of course they were vindictive, and that was the fault of Germany's ruthlessness after 1870. But we had no such excuse. Only we had Grey. Possibly any other cabinet minister would have been as bad; anyhow our crime is manifestly greater than Germany's and France's because it is without even the vestige of an excuse. There was absolutely no reason in the nature of things why we should make France our favourites rather than Germany. We had recently been bullying France, and then it amused us to be friends with her and then with Russia. And so we chose the darkness instead of the light, not knowing of course what we were doing but trusting cabinet ministers and foreign office fools, who are really the least trustworthy people in the world, their principles being always without exception wrong. Of course once we took sides, things went from bad to worse, and Germany gradually became more and more desperate, seeing Russia grow-ing stronger, and with the added menace of our support to the unholy alliance. About our subservience to Russia I can't feel calmly. I see reptiles like Wells defend Russian tyranny now. I suppose the Czar is now going to be our national hero, naturally, since we have gone to war at his bidding. For that at least is certain. There can be no doubt in any fair minded person's mind that it was the Czar not the Kaiser who directly caused the war by his mobilisation. But the ultimate question was a different one; rather was Germany a menace to Euro-pean civilisation? Well, I say if, and in so far as it was, then we had done our best to make it so. France and Germany were both tarred with the same brush, and I fear we were too, less black perhaps, but with far less excuse. No, look at it whatever way one tries, the German-menace-to-Europe theory breaks down, the moment one tries to induce those who believe in the theory to support it by argument – just as the English – or the French-menace theory would break down if one pushed a German holder of such a theory. The Russian menace is another matter. Despite Wells and such curs, I believe it to be a real one; how great, time only will show. You yourself have warned us of it, in your splendid and timely letter. But seeing that so clearly, as you did, and no doubt still must do, can you really be partially blind to the full consequences? It is true that history is never simple, but only too misleadingly complex; but you as an historian can hardly be misled as to the dominant fact, which is not German arrogance, or German desire for bigamony, but German fear of Russia, and therefore of

Russia's friends. The Belgium matter is surely only a magnified instance (greatly magnified no doubt) of military bad manners in a people fighting for its life. I cannot believe you can be deceived by it, as Papa is; and others who are unable to see more than one side of a polygon at once. No more can you be taken in by the obligation-to-France theory, which is solely based on Grey's falsehoods. It must, I suppose, be the German menace theory that prevents you from going on as you began, and supporting those few who are fighting for light against darkness. Courage is the last thing you lack, and it must be some scruple of conscience. But can you seriously believe that Germany should be crushed? Why not France? They are both guilty, and in any belief equally. I can't myself pose as a champion of this cause, because, alas, I have never trained myself to write effectively, except possibly in verse, which cannot be written for the purposes of the moment. But you are a writer, as influential as any in the country, and that is why I am so sad, that having begun so nobly, you are pausing now, when you might be leading all that is best in English thought out of this miserable nightmare jungle of confused and futile puzzlement and disgust. So if I have written all these pages of muddled incoherent stuff, which others have put far more effectively and the gist of which must be perfectly familiar to you, – you will quite understand why I am sure. Anyhow there is nothing else to say it seems to me, only it can be put better or worse, and I wish you could make up your mind to put some of it at least, as only you would do. – One word more. Doubtless blame must be distributed all round, if we are to [be] impartial; and one will lay the greater burden on one country, and another on another. You, say, on Germany, I on Russia. But it is, as I see it, our absolute duty to put all the weight of blame earned by our country upon her, as outspokenly and fearlessly as possible, not sparing her in the least, whether or not we think her blame is proportionally greater or less than that of others. After all, who but we English can effectually lesson England, and save her from worse things? And how except by telling her the truth? But apart from the duty of convincing our-selves of sin, there is the future to think of and to work for, as Charles and others are doing. Conviction of sin is necessary to repentance; but the fruits of repentance are doubtless more important than conviction of sin. Only they won't come by mere praying. But I am preaching, and must stop. What I have written expresses the opinion we both, B. and I, hold very strongly; and you of course understand no one has asked me to write, or knows I am doing so.

Yours affectionately,

R.C.T.

On World War 1.

2, Cheyne Gardens,
S.W.
Aug. 28, 1914.

Dear Bob,

I am sure if, it comes to writing, nothing could be better than your letter which moved me very much. I am really too broken in spirit to attempt to answer it properly and indeed the mugwump is not morally in a position to hold his own against either side. He feels a self contempt when he compares himself to his whole hearted friends. I never admired Charles more, nor those who are standing with him. I think, further, that they have a most useful part to perform, if they keep within measure as they are at present doing.

But I am not inclined to go further with them myself at present, thinking (as half of my friends I find think also) something as follows.

1. I think being in it we must win this war, or Germany (enraged to death with us) will plant herself as overlord of Western Europe and design our overthrow under highly favourable conditions. This particuliar proposition, whether agreed to or not, is irrespective of the question of how we got into the war. Being in it I think we *must* win, and I am very keen on the enlisting going well in order to win without conscription. So I don't feel inclined to say all I think against our policy, as I want people to be hearty to win the war, which I think will be very difficult, – especially as people are evidently at soul horror-struck by the whole enormous catastrophe of civilization. There is no jingoism as in the Boer war. I don't think we can afford to discourage ourselves further, if we are to survive at all.

2. I do feel quite differently from you and Charles about Belgium. I think and feel about it just as the ordinary pro-war people: – the heroism of the Belgians thrills me, the brutal contempt of public law in building railways years ago in malice prepense to pass through a guaranteed neutral state that had done the invaders no harm, seems to me the sort of thing that gives us fair warning of what Europe will be like if these Zabernists become the dominant power.

3. I care rather more for France than you do. I am sure the German nation and culture and soul can survive a beating and may *possibly* be the better for it, though as to that I am not as confident as most people. But at any rate it can survive. But if France has another 1870 I think the disillusionment and

pessimism of the French soul will be immensely increased, they will never hold up their heads again in any sense – also Germany will certainly take measures to prevent their ever having diplomatic independence again. The prospect of Germany bleeding France white again and planting herself as overlord of the West is one that not even my great fear of Russia can overcome.

4. I object to the *entente* as I have always done. It is as bad (at least) as alliance, and the system of alliances have been the cause of this universal catastrophe arising out a genuine local quarrel between Austria, Russia and Serbia about the South Slavs in Austro-Hungary, (on which question by the way I sympathize with the Slavs on grounds of nationality as in the affair of Italy sixty years ago). The *entente* was as bad as possible. What I think we ought to have done for the last eight years was to be neutral and friendly to both France and Germany, but to tell these Germans long ago that if they violated Belgium we should fight them, and leave them to lay their plans accordingly. Considering as I do that a second overwhelming of France by Germany was a calamity of the worst sort, I think it behoved us at least to see that the Germans fought fair and did not invade France through a country she and we had guaranteed. Germany was prepared to turn that innocent country into the scene of all these horrors, which would have occurred there *even if the Belgians had not resisted*, unless you assume that the Germans would have marched straight into Paris which is

1. not certain
2. not desirable – as a result of the violation of public law in the case of Belgium.

5. As to Russia, I fully realize the danger of her ending up as the strongest power. But Germany's dominance of the true Western countries is a more pressing and locally nearer danger now that she has gone through Belgium. The prospect is profoundly gloomy, whoever wins this war, but it may be a little less bad if we can help to save France instead of leaving her either to be again trampled out of all respect, or else to be lifted out of the ditch solely by Russia.

It must also be remembered that, at present, large Slav communities are subject to Teutons, and infamously treated by them; it must be our part to see that if we win the war no Teuton communities are subjected to Slavs.

The Germans are no doubt afraid of the Slavs; I sympathize deeply with that fear, but I am bound to say their means of protecting themselves against it have been to say the least, unfortunate:- viz.

1. The Partition of Poland, their natural barrier.
2. The land policy, in Prussian Poland in the last generation, going back to our 17th century methods in Ireland. That and Zabern must not be forgotten when we consider what a Prussian conquest of France and Belgium would mean.
3. By way of protecting themelves from Russia they have withdrawn their army from the Russian border and flung it into a friendly, highly civilized little state in the West with a view to 'bleeding France white', by a violation of public law.

I admire Charles and his friends, and agree with much of what they say and I think someone should say it – though cautiously at present. But I don't think it is any more the *whole* truth than the Wells★ point of view, in spite of the fact that Charles, Morel†, Macdonald and Norman Angel‡ are each of them worth 20 of Wells, and all that he writes on the subject makes me sick. I may be going out to Greece and the Balkans early next week with Noel Banton and Basil Williams§ – where England is trying to reconstitute the Xtian Balkan League which was so tragically shattered by the last war. In a sense one feels it hardly matters what one does or thinks in this doomsday. However much you disagree with what I have written, believe that I am absolutely heartbroken and think it far the greatest catastrophe in modern history, and that my feeling about Sartor passage is even stronger than it was. But as long as you have devils like the Russians and German militarist parties in being, and in *power*, can the rest of the world adopt complete passivism and survive? But there I am arguing again. I want to end up saying how much I admire your letter and respect your attitude and despise my own – but I can't help it.

Yours affectionately
George.

★Herbert George Wells (1866–1946), journalist, historian, author.
†Edmund Morel (1873–1924), author & journalist; Labour MP,1922–24; editor of *Africa Mail*,1903–15; vice president of Anti-Slavery Society.
‡Sir Norman Angel (1872–1967); publicist; works include: *The Great Illusion*,1910; Nobel Peace Prize,1933
§Basil Williams (1867–1950); historian; major work: The *Whig Supremacy, 1714–60* (1939).

2.

2, Cheyne Gardens,
S.W.
Aug. 31, 1914.

Dear Bob,

I am sorry I wrote you a long argumentative letter, not a very good one. My real position in brief is that I 'think' Grey and Asquith's committals to France in making war plans behind our backs years ago and concealing it was very wrong indeed; but that the invasion of Belgium made it both just and necessary for us to fight.

The two propositions are not contradictory, though it is possible to disagree with either. The destruction of Louvain greatly increases my intense desire to prevent the Germans becoming the overlords of Western Europe, this would I think lower civilisation, and render our own position untenable for long. I am not going to Serbia now, as the route across France has suddenly become dangerous and another Balkan war is threatened in Serbia's rear. I may go later if things ever get better. Julian looks very well and jolly. The Russian mobilization is pleaded as an excuse for all this. It was no doubt the cause, but not the justification. And the Russian mobilization may equally well be excused as the only way of stopping Austria from overrunning Serbia which she was actually *doing* when Russia mobilized, being at war with Serbia after an ultimatum of 48 hours to Serbia which was meant to bring on war. I do not think our people have been blameless. I think the *entente* as wrong as I always thought it, and the Russian *entente* in particular quite wrong, and morally degrading. But I think we are on the right side and that we must win or the world will be far worse than it was before, and *even* worse than it will be when we have won!

How I envy children, for they only think 10 minutes a day about the war! It is the shipwreck of civilization.

Yours ever,
George.

On joining the Serbian Relief Fund.

2, Cheyne Gardens,
S.W.
Dec. 14, 1914

Dear Bob,

Seton Watson and I start for Serbia tomorrow. We are going out for the Serbian Relief Fund to enquire into the best way of spending a portion of its funds. And it is just the time for the few Englishmen who have any connections with Serbia to put in an appearance there.

I shall be gone by the time this reaches you so there is no use writing. But I just wanted to say goodbye and good luck to you and Bessie and Julian. We shall be back in about two months.

Your affectionate brother,
George.

1915

More on the War.

> 21, East Eleventh Street,
> New York.
> May 21, 1915.

Dear Jackson★,

Your kind letter of May 4 reached me in the U.S. where I have been lecturing on Serbia and the war there; I was in Serbia in the winter, and the U.S. people have been exceedingly generous in aiding the misery in Serbia. It was very interesting being here during the great outburst of wrath on the sinking of the *Lusitania*.† The Bryce Report came out the next day. Truly we are fighting savages who will destroy us if they win and the issue is in doubt. I used to think you wrong about general military training, but I don't now.

I fear I must persist in my resignation from the Ad Iundem, though with the warmest feelings towards its members especially towards you. Italy's *soul* has conquered her baser part, represented by the political 'boss' Giolitti‡. Mazzini§ has triumphed over Machiavelli.¶ If I felt as sure of military victory to follow I should wholly rejoice.

I return to England tomorrow.

> Yrs truly
> G.M. Trevelyan,

★Sir Francis Jackson (1870–1947); educated at Harrow & Trin. Coll. Camb.; well-known cricketer and administrator; close friend of the Trevelyans.

†*Lusitania*: unarmed passenger ship under British registration, sunk off the Irish coast by a German submarine on 7 May 1915; 1,195 persons lost their lives, of whom 128 were U.S. citizens.

‡Giovanni Giolitti (1842–1928); Italian politicians; five times prime minister of Italy between 1892 and 1921.

§Giuseppe Mazzini (1805–1872); an outstanding Italian patriot, revolutionist; political and social writer.

¶Niccolo Machiavelli (1469–1527); Italian author and statesman; his best known work: *The Prince* (1532).

On the fate of the Finns.

Reggio. Calabria.

Dear Bob,

Thank you very much for your letter. I have been and am greatly troubled about the Finns. I saw Reuter (the Finnish Reuter) at the time he was moving about the Pollock in Westlake circular and I gave him some hints about it, e.g. to go to Pollock, which he followed, and we agreed that *then* it would be worse than useless for my Ponsonby* lot to move, beyond publishing the pamphlet in the name of the Parliamentary Committee, which we forthwith did. *Now* perhaps we, or one of us, ought to do more if no one else will do anything. I will give the matter attention the moment I get to town and see what protest, if any, it will be best to make. Of course we cannot save the Finns, only Grey if he tried hard could make any difference, and he won't. But no doubt some protest should be made. It is the worst thing since the 2nd partition of Poland.

Yrs ever,
George.

I am glad to hear such a good account of Julian. I reach London on the night of the 5th, as soon as this.

---

*Arthur Ponsonby (1871–1946); politician & author; a lifelong pacifist, urging negotiated peace throughout the War of 1914–18; Liberal MP, 1908-18.

On Bob's poem *Krishna*.

British Red Cross Society

London Office,   Croce Rossa Britannica,
123 Pall Mall, S.W.   Primo Sezione
                                        S. Giovanni di Manzano,
                                        Udine,
                                        Italy.
                                        May 3 1917.

Dear Bob,

Thank you very much for *Krishna*. I read it in the first day of real Italian summer yesterday with very great delight, and found it very refreshing to the spirit. It has a 'mental atmosphere' of its own – not Indian or anything else, – in which the whole story and poem moves which gives it originality and success. Also the metre, to which I am very sensitive, though I am very ignorant of its mysteries, is very fine and variegated. I have been reading a lot of Milton lately and appreciate metre, especially your work which has relation to the Miltonic metres, very much.

I am now proceeding to read the rest of the book.

Best love to Bessie and Julian.

Your aff. brother,
George.

P.S. Did you invent the story?

1918

Letters from Italy.

1.

British Red Cross Society

London office: Croce Rossa Britannica
15 Strand, W.C. 2.   Prima Sezione
                                                          Intendenda III Armata
                                                          Zona di Guerra.

Oct. 24, 1918

Dear Bob,

Thanks for the paper re Molly's money which I have signed and sent back to Sir Hugh Bell★.

I was very glad to get your letter saying where you were and exactly what you were doing. Surely the long armistice time, whenever that may begin, will be just when your people's work will come in more than ever. And a library if well chosen may be very much to the point.

I am sorry to hear about Bas. Meyer's brother's death. If you see Bas. Meyer remember me to him and tell him *we hope to get the Star lorry on the road again before demobilization.* He will understand.

We have had a quiet year this year, except for the one week in June. But I've got back to writing work now and am by no means dull, between that and reading the papers – and the beauty of the sub Alps and Luganeans at any time of year is in itself a resource.

Yours ever,
George Trevelyan.

We are within 2 miles of Petrarch's† house at this base of ours. It is a most genuine affair – as genuine as the house at Stratford, and the cat that was in his room when he died in his chair reading is stuffed over the door of the room!

★Charles P. Trevelyan married 1904 Mary, daughter of Sir Hugh Bell, 2nd Bart.
†Francesco Petrarch (1304–1374); Italian poet & humanist; great figure in Italian literature.

2.

British Red Cross Society

London Office: Croce Rossa Britannica
15 Strand, W.C.2.   Prima Sezione
                                                 Intendenda III Armata
                                                 Zona di Guerra
                                                 Nov. 12, 1918.

Dear Bob,

Thank you very much for yours of Nov. 5 and for forwarding Pease's letter. I have spoken to Edwardes and I think it quite possible that he and Sykes* may go back to the Fr. War Victims Relief work in France when we break up, which will I hope be quite early next year. I have asked Edwardes to speak to anyone of our number whom […]†. and suitable so that they could make an offer of their services to Mr Harvey when the time comes. Please assure Mr Harvey that I will do all I can to help in the matter, though of course no one can go until this Unit breaks up, and that date is still unfixed. If Mr Harvey or you can send us any up to date literature or statement about your recent and prospective work, or anything as to what sort of people e.g. driver, mechanics, secretaries, or what not required, it would help. I feel rather in the dark as to what the service of most of your members individually consists in, though I understand the general nature of the work. Also whether it is all voluntary unpaid.

Yours ever
George

*Sir Frederick Sykes (1877–1954); Chief of Airstaff, 1918–19.
†Illegible writing.

1920

On reading Bob's *Lucretius*.

Trinity College,
Cambridge.
Aug. 24, 1920.

Dear Bob,

Thank you very much indeed for the *Lucretius*. I have read the greater part of it now and look forward much to the rest. The impression left on me more than a year ago of its excellence when you gave me a taste of it up at the Lake Hunt, is fully confirmed. It is an admirable combination of *clearness* of meaning (where clearness is very difficult to secure) with dignity of style. Of its scholarship I can say nothing, but that I imagine there is no doubt of.

What a wonderful old bird Lucretius was, – and
'*est, ut ante, carus*'.

Your affectionate brother
George.

1921

GMT to his father George Otto on the funeral of the latter's close friend.

Trinity College,
Cambridge.
Common room. 6.p.m.
Sep. 28, 1921.

I came here for Jackson's funeral this morning and am going back tonight. I came for you as well as for myself. I can hardly say that any of his real contemporaries were here. But, save for that negative witness to the great age he had reached, it could not have been a more beautiful and impressive ceremony. It was vacation so a beautiful quiet reigned in the College and the town; but the Fellows and Former Fellows were there in real strength, probably about 50, or near it. We met in the cloisters and formed a column, in twos, behind the coffin under Wren's library, and followed him, (headed by the Master) out into Trinity Lane by Garrett Hostel Gate, and in to the College again by the Queen's Gate from Trinity Lane, where the other attendant members of the University, more numerous than ourselves, formed in column behind us. And so we all followed him across the Great Court into the Chapel, where half the service took place. Then, in the same order, we followed him out across the Great Court, still in brilliant autumn sunshine; – and so he left the College for the last time. Some of us, including myself, walked out, (others driving) to the cemetery on the edge of the town, where, close to Jebb and Verrall, we left him, under a pine tree, in the breath of the country itself. His sons and daughters were also present.

Parry, whom I have since talked to, was very much pleased with it all; and indeed, inasmuch as he died at Bournemouth, after having been several weeks with his wife, there has been nothing painful except that the best of men are as the grass of the field.

Your affectionate son,
George.

1922

On reading Bob's *Oresteia*.

> Pen Rose,
> Berkhamsted.
> Dec. 23, 1922.

Dear Bob,

I'm deep in the *Oresteia*. The sense that one can trust the scholarship and the faithfulness to the word and the spirit of the Greek adds greatly to the pleasure of the high and dignified verse, and to the lyrical qualities. Thank you very much indeed for sending it me. It makes a lovely Xmas present and Xmas reading. I do wish you and Bessie could manage to come here for a weekend in Feb. before we go to Italy. It's a long time since we've had a talk.

> Your aff. brother
> George.

1923

Thanking Bob for his editorial help.

Garden Corner,
West Road,
Cambridge.
Oct. 12, 1923

Dear Bob,

Thank you very much for your marks. I have adopted your few suggestions with gratitude. I enclose my copy of excerpts from G.O.T's letters to you (which I have here). Will you read them and return them with any comments? I intend to print them at the end of the text of the memoir, and before the *Horace at Athens* etc. if you have no objection.

I am so glad C.A. is better. I agree with him that the P.M. is cutting the best and most dignified figure of the lot. Whether that will save our unfortunate country and world remains to be seen. '*Sherianeo*' as the Italians say.

Yrs. ever,
G.M.T.

On the future of Italy.

The Athenaeum,
Pall Mall, S.W. 1.
Oct. 26, 1923.

Dear Bob,

I'm very glad you think well of Manin*, for your judgements are among those I really value. It was very jolly of you to read it aloud and I am glad it stood the test.

There is indeed a vast amount to be said and thought about the 'federal' question – the more so now that united Italy is in many ways a disappointment with the break down of free government. Only I am certain of one thing – neither the south nor centre of Italy could have established and maintained free government, or even civilized government without the north to help it. Also on the whole I think the union was inevitable in the end because there were no real provincial patriotisms (except the Piedmontese) to make real states of, so that Federalism would only have meant further disturbance and civil war. No federal system could have been strong enough to abolish the temporal power. Similarly I don't believe that if Germany is now broken up into States it will not come together again some day.

Yours ever
George.

---

*Daniele Manin (1804–1857), Venetian statesman; liberal leader. GMT wrote his life: *Manin and the Venetian Revolution of 1848* (1923).

1924

On reading Bob's *Antigone*.

Pen Rose,
Berkhamsted.
Dec. 9, 1924.

Dear Bob,

I have had a delightful Sunday morning reading the *Antigone*, and Humphry★ has been looking at it with great interest as he has just been doing the original at school. It seems excellent and successful in just the way of your *Oresteia*. I hope it also will be acted in Old Sarum!

Thank you very much indeed. Love to Bessie and to Julian when he comes home.

Yrs. ever,
George.

★GMT's son.

1925

A note to Bob's wife, Bessie.

The Athenaeum,
Pall Mall,
S.W.1.
June 8, 1925.

Dear Bessie,

We were delighted to get your letter this morning. How very interesting that your life should have been exactly into 2 parts of 25. I enjoyed Holland so very much at Easter and your friends were so kind to us. It has left a great picture and impression on my mind, as well as on the perhaps more impressionable virgin soil of Mary's. I also greatly enjoyed meeting Bob at the Hunt and reading his book of poetic criticism. Please both take our dear loves and live another 25 years till Julian is a very distinguished architect. Three rounds of 25 is all I ask for myself or others.

Yours ever
George.

On Bob's *Theocritus*.

> Pen Rose,
> Berkhamsted.
> Nov. 12, 1925.

Dear Bob,

I gave your *Theocritus* to my father-in-law on his 80th birthday, and he has been going through it with the Greek and is full of admiration of it and asks me to send you his compliments on it.

We are having a great business here saving some of the wonderful Ashridge wilderness for the National Trust. We have got at least £40000 worth – a magnificent estate, tho' only a part of the whole.

> Yrs ever,
> George.

1926

A note to Bessie.

> Pen Rose,
> Berkhamsted.
> July 28, 1926.

Dear Bessie,

Thanks for your card. I am glad there is a duplicate. I will keep the text and bring it round with me to Northumberland. I have read it and am most enthusiastic. I read Motley's account afterwards – the internal situation and politics inside Leyden seem not to have been known to Motley. The two accounts supplement each other splendidly. Geyl★ has sent me his notes – very good I think – but incomplete. I have sent them back to him, with one or two very small suggestions.

I will write the Preface after seeing you at the end of Aug. and him at the end of Sept.

> Yrs ever,
> George.

★Pietr Geyl, Dutch historian, major works: *The Revolt of the Netherlands, 1555–1609; The Netherlands in the Seventeenth Century, 1609–48*.

Thanking Bob for his editorial help.

Pen Rose,
Berkhamsted.
Oct. 27, 1926.

Dear Bob,

Thank you very much for your letter. The corrections I have already sent on this morning to Longmans', though they will be just too late for a reprint completing this week. I am glad you find the Victorian part was tolerable. The 'epilogue' – imposed on me much against my will by the Publisher's view of necessity, I believe a correct view – could not be anything but a blot. I don't understand the age we live in, and what I do understand I don't like.

Mary is 'enjoying herself fine' in Holland, and I believe her attachment will be permanent. Bessie's introductions have made a great difference to her happiness there.

Yrs ever,
G.M.T.

1927

On reading Bob's *Meleager*.

Welcombe,
Stratford on Avon
March 13, 1927

Dear Bob,

I have just read your *Meleager*, on a quiet weekend here. I read it with real excitement. I think it has great power and romance and originality, besides that careful artistry we are accustomed to in your work. The contrast of the morning youth and beauty of the first scene with the tragedy of the second is very fine. I don't know where you got the idea of the ghosts from – I suppose you invented it. It is very effective. Having the central events of the story and all the secondary characters save one kept *off* the stage gives concentration to the personal tragedy of Meleager and Atalanta.

I am glad you brought in the family motto, which is the best family motto I know.

Mary enjoyed herself very much with you and Bessie at The Shiffolds.

Yrs ever
G.M.T.

On the *No Plays*.

36, Chelsea Park Gardens,
S.W.3.
March 17, 1927.

Dear Bob,

I am deeply interested in what you tell me about the *No Plays*, I think the adaptation has been most successful. By means of making the ghosts *repeat* the passions of the previously enacted drama, it was rendered possible to omit the scene depicting the tragedy itself, which has been done so often and involves so many characters that it was desirable to omit it provided this could be done without omitting the whole passion of the piece.

Yrs ever
G.M.T.

On being appointed as Regius Professor History at Cambridge.

Pen Rose,
Berkhamsted.
June 16, 1927.

Dear Bob,

The P.M. has asked me to go to Cambridge and I have accepted. The K's pleasure has still to be taken, so until it is announced it is a secret, and please will you and Bessie treat it as such till it is in the papers. I have been down to Cambridge, and by permission talked to the 2 or 3 principal history dons there, with satisfactory results, as to what I can do and what need not do there. Queen Anne will move more slowly, but she will move. We shall probably transfer our household in there about January, when we have got a house. We go to Robin Ghyll★ on Wed. 20th and stay there till Aug. 25 when we go on to Cambo, I shall have the fun of writing an Inaugural Lecture up in the North. I have got the first rent payment (£75) today and next week shall get another £50 from the Hallington Estate. In a few weeks I hope to get *about* £300 (non-recurrent) residue of the personal estate left after death duties, legal expenses, etc. I have therefore today ordered Drummonds to transfer £50 to your account, and when the £200 comes in I will order them to pay another £50, – making £100 for this first year. In later years the rent may not come up to £300, and in that case I shall only pay ⅓ of whatever it is. But that will at least amount to £70 a year.

Best love to you all from your aff. brother

G.M. Trevelyan.

★ Family cottage in Langdale.

On Bob's classical plays.

Trinity College,
Cambridge.
Oct. 30, 1927.

Dear Bob,

I like *Cheiron* very much indeed and shall be proud of the dedication. I am very much *interested* in your latest classical plays. They take me into a world of moral, intellectual and aesthetic imagination which is altogether pleasant to me. And without directly setting out to criticize real life, they actually do so. I delight in them.

Yrs affectionately
George.

1928

On living at Welcombe.

> Garden Corner,
> West Road,
> Cambridge.
> Jan. 24, 1928

Dear Bob,

I enclose a letter from Aunt Annie which I beg you to read carefully.

When you have read it allow me to add these suggestions on my own account. If you feel disposed to write to Papa at once in the sense she suggests, I should begin by saying that you do not know whether dear Mama is really likely to leave us quite soon or not. But that you understand from Aunt Annie that it is a possibility. That if so you are most anxious that Papa should not take any steps for leaving Welcombe in the near future. That Aunt Annie does not at all like the idea of his going north till the warm weather, and is alarmed about it. That you share this view that if dear Mama is taken from us you will have much to say to him, and that there will be many plans to talk out, which had much better be done at leisure at Welcombe, and that you earnestly hope he will make no arrangement for leaving it.

I would not say anything definite about his *permanently* living at Welcombe, because we all desire that should be conditional, and the time for mentioning the condition is not yet. But you might perhaps add that you have no thought of moving into Welcombe yourselves as an additional reason for his staying there at least at present.

You will judge how much of this you think fit to say. But such is my advice. I would be careful to write of Mama's death as a possibility only. But in view of Aunt Annie's letter I think the time has come for you to write something.

> Yrs ever,
> George.

To Bessie on George Otto's papers.

Garden Corner,
West Road,
Cambridge.
June 15, 1928.

Dear Bessie,

I am very glad the high backed chairs sold so well.

I fear poor dear Papa, owing to his debility, has made rather a mess about the papers in the bureau to which you refer. He sent for me to tell me – I went all the way up to Northumberland because he said he had something very important to tell me at once. I was able to do some Hallington business too, so it was all right. But the thing he had to tell me was that there were his papers that were to be mine when he died. And he wanted to give me the key. But, when he came to look for it he couldn't find it! So that's that, and unless you want to remove the bureau at once, I think we must leave things as they are till his death.

I am so glad of your good news about Julian.

Yrs ever,
George.

On the future location of books left by George Otto Trevelyan.

Hallington Hall,
Newcastle-on-Tyne,
22 miles.)
Aug. 10, 1928.

Dear Bob,

I have been considering at leisure the books left to me in Papa's Will*, and have come to the conclusion that one set would be very much better as yours than as mine and I beg you to accept it. I refer to the collection of the Latin Classics of Pipontine or Deux Pont Edition, in old white binding, over 100 vols. in all, now in the two side sections of the glass bookshelf in Papa's study. Many of the volumes have notes by Macaulay which we should equally appreciate in so far as they are Macaulay's, but which you will appreciate and understand far better than I because they are on points of classical scholarship and history in which I am an ignoramus. Nothing would give me greater pleasure than to think of them as occupying a place in the new Library at the Shiffolds, and as being often taken down from the shelf by you.

Give me the great pleasure of contributing towards the initiation of the new Shiffold library.

Your affectionate brother,
George.

★George Otto Trevelyan died in August 1928.

With regard to the Macaulay journals.

Garden Corner,
West Road,
Cambridge.
Nov. 20, 1928.

Dear Bob,

I am glad to hear from Charles that the Name and Arms are dead.
The enclosed may interest you: I should be obliged if you would return it.

Yours ever
G.M.T.

P.S. I have read nearly all the Macaulay Journals and have come to the conclusion that it would be a mistake to make an extensive publication of them. Papa with great skill extracted the best parts. The rest is interesting, much of it, if one really cares about Macaulay, but was never meant by him for publication but only for his own amusement in re-reading it.

1929

On the engagement of GMT's daughter Mary to John Moorman.

Robin-Ghyll,
Langdale,
Ambleside.
Sep. 30, 1929

Dear Bob and Bessie,

As we have hoped and expected for some weeks past, Mary is engaged to be married to John Moorman* who was at Hallington for a week in August. He has only known her since June, when they met at the Cornford's musical parties at Cambridge. He is just her age and only left Cambridge this year. He stayed on there after his degree to train for a clergyman. He is now a curate in Leeds. He is a fine scholar, has studied medieval documents under Coulton who thinks highly of him, and belongs as much to the academic as to the clerical world. His *views* are liberal-minded, and I have talked about religion and history with him with much agreement and no feeling of barrier such as I should feel with a narrow-minded parson – or an Anglo Catholic even – is not narrow minded. He is a fine walker and has walked his fifty miles. He Is small but wiry. His father was Professor of English at Leeds, but was drowned some years ago by accident. His mother, much respected in academic circles, is matron of a hall of some kind in the University there. The most intimate friend of the family is Grant who recently retired from the History Professorship there; he is a first-rate man, very much of my persuasion. Among John Moorman's most intimate elder and younger friends are Bishop of Wyld whom you remember at our parents' funeral, and his son. In fact Moorman's whole entourage and atmosphere is about equally academic and clerical – and both of a very good type. I know enough of him to think he will suit Mary very well, and enough of her to think that not many people would. So Janet and I are very much pleased indeed.

Your aff. brother,
George.

*Mary Caroline Moorman (1905–1994); GMT's daughter (Mary Trevelyan); married in 1930 Rev. John Moorman (1905–1989) afterwards Bishop of Ripon,1959–75. Major works by John Moorman: *A History of the Church in England* (1953); *Vatican Observed* (1967).

Would Welcombe remain unspoiled?

> Garden Corner,
> West Road,
> Cambridge.
> Nov. 19, 1929.

My Dear Bessie,

I am very much afraid that I am so exceedingly busy now that I cannot undertake to read Dr Renier's work. I am sorry.

There is one thing that I do not know about the interesting Welcombe situation. Does Flower's purchase include the dingles and little wooded valleys exactly opposite the windows of the large Hall and the two entrance doors of Welcombe, the other side of the footpath? That is, to me, more than the Warwick road, the really sacred place, the unspoiled *Welcombe* where Shakespeare undoubtedly roamed and where he bought the tithe. I always hoped that would not be sold in Villa lots and suggested some arrangement about it. Withers said it must go with the House, which might otherwise be unsaleable. I hope therefore it *has* gone with the House, and is in no danger of being sold separately and cut up for bungalows.

> Yours affectionately
> George.

1930

Thanking Bessie for her help.

Garden Corner,
West Road,
Cambridge.

Heidelberg.
April 6, 1930.

Dear Bessie,

Your letter and enclosures reached me abroad, where Mary and I have had a very nice 4 days at the Hague, where I found a large number of Marlborough's letters to Heinsius in the Archives there. Janet has now joined us and we are going on to Blenheim.

It was a kind thought of you to send me those old papers. The one on Pitt was not of much interest, but I am very glad to have the other. It is a real historical curiosity, being the famous pamphlet exhorting to the assassination of Cromwell, entitled 'Killing no Murder'. I may have it bound when I get home.

So it is the last of Welcombe at length!

I hope it won't become a Popery-hole – but what must be must and the other aspect of the affair is most satisfactory. I am so glad it is off your hands.

Yours ever
George.

1931

On visiting Belgium.

Garden Corner,
West Road,
Cambridge.
March 25, 1931.

Dear Bessie,

I am very sorry to hear Bob has this troublesome operation. But I suppose it will be nothing more than troublesome being thus taken in good time.

The 'Welcombe Hotel' is advertising itself already I hear. I shall go and stay there a night some day. I think it is such a good thing.

That reminds me that being in Belgium last week viewing the battlefields at Ramillies and Oudenarde, I went in to the Beaux Arts at Brussels, and suddenly and unexpectedly found myself looking at the Welcombe Memling – it is Memling, is it not – the 2 donors? A nice bearded, gentlemanly looking man was making a copy of it, and I asked him if it was a new picture. 'O yes,' he said 'it was bought by the "friends of the Belgian arts" – or some such body – for the gallery for a fabulous sum!' I told him I was very glad it was there in the country of its origin, instead of America. It looked very well, though in a room with other good pictures – not so good I think.

Yrs ever,
George.

On having written a memoir of his father George Otto Trevelyan

Hallington Hall,
Newcastle-on-Tyne.
(22 miles.)
Sept. 9, 1931

Dear Bob,

I have just received a letter from Withers saying that you will pay me £ 1500, which will in fact be very useful to me at this moment. Thank you very much indeed. It is a very pleasant aftermath to the whole of our family business that began four years ago.

I have just completed a short memoir of Papa – about 45000 words – which I propose to publish next spring unless the country has been ruined by then and publishing is impossible★.

I have had 3 copies made and shall put one into C.P.T.'s hands, and propose to send one to you whenever you can give attention – at once if you wish it now. Do you think you could read it and mark anything, great or small, about which you would like to speak to me? And could you come down some weekend to Cambridge in Oct. (barring Oct. 26) to talk about it? Or would you prefer me to come to the Shiffolds for a couple of nights before term begins – possibly the weekend Oct 3–5?

Your aff. bro.
George.

★The book was published under the title: *Sir Geoge Otto Trevelyan: A Memoir* (1932).

On having arranged a cheap edition of George Otto Trevelyan's
Life of Macaulay.

R.C. Trevelyan Esq   Garden Corner,
The Shiffolds,   West Road,
Holmbury St. Mary,   Cambridge.
nr. Dorking.   Oct. 22, 1931.

Many thanks. I am glad you approve. The italics represented Papa's underlinings, and the other words were as he wrote them. But I shall underline *excédés*, and put *being* for *be*.

I have arranged for a cheap ed. of Papa's *Life of Macaulay* to be brought out by the Oxford Press in their Worlds Classics series. Nelson's cheap ed. sold out some years ago and there is only Longmans' expensive ed.

G.M.T.

1934

Thanking Bob for his editorial help.

Garden Corner,
West Road, Cambridge.
March 21, 1934

Dear Bob,

It always gives me the greatest pleasure to get your letters about my books, for I think you are perhaps better qualified to judge them *as books* than anyone else.

Your corrections and suggestions are also, always so useful and interesting.

Your readings of Pope's Prologue are clearly improvements. I took my text from an early copy of the *play*, but Pope must have made the alterations or corrections you give.

'First famed Cato' is better, but 'first-named' might have been the original clumsier way of designating Cato the Censor. p.127 of lines from bottom should read

'she did *so* only to avoid'

Seconded is a usual term to lending a soldier into temporary civil employment, or lending any person in one office to fulfil another function without actually vacating his permanent office.

p.123 the Norfolk Squire is Walpole.

Our best love to Bessie.

Yours ever affectionately,
George

On a new selection of Bob's poems.

Garden Corner,
West Road,
Cambridge.
Dec. 7, 1934.

Dear Bob,

As a matter of fact I am not on the board of electors for the Italian Professorship this time.

I have just read the Macmillan selection of your poems with very great pleasure. They were nearly all old friends but read very well indeed together. I hear about Bessie's eyes etc. from Janet. I do hope you will both be spared serious distress in that way.

Love to you both.

Yrs ever affectionately
George.

I keep dreaming these nights that we three brothers are playing soldiers again on the floor. I always get tremendously excited about it.

An appreciation of Bob's poems.

Address till Jan. 9,   Garden Corner,
Hallington Hall,   West Road,
Newcastle on Tyne.   Cambridge.
                                              Dec. 14, 1934.

Dear Bob,

I gave your (Macmillan's) Selected Poems to A.E. Housman★ here, who replies:

'Many thanks for sending me your brother's poems, in which I admire as usual the absence of the vices usually present in poetry: no strain or false intensity or merely external glitter. I rather think that the best piece in the book is *Winter Rain*.'

A happy Xmas to you and Bessie.

Your aff. brother,
G.M.T.

★Alfred Edward Housman (1859–1936); poet & classical scholar; professor of Latin, Cambridge, 1911–36.

1935

A personal note to Bob.

Hallington Hall,
Newcastle-on-Tyne.
(22 miles.)
Xmas eve, 1935.

Dear Bob,

It makes me sad that we have seen so little of each other lately, and that I have seen so little of Bessie. I am so very sorry indeed that her eyesight is not better. If I may, I will visit the Shiffolds in the Easter vacation if you are there. And could you stay with Janet and me some weekend next term? We should be delighted to have you any time you could come.

It is a real Xmas up here this year, with a hard long frost and snow. Janet and I are alone here – Janet *quite* well of her eczema now – but within reach of the cheerful party at Wallington, so that we are very happy as we both like to be quiet sometimes especially up here.

Your affectionate brother,
George.

1936

On the ultimate destination of the Macaulay classics.

Hallington Hall,
Newcastle-on-Tyne,
(22 miles.)
July 29, 1936.

Dear Bob,

Yes, things seem to be going better in the Wallington family. Molly is very grateful to you. Your kind suggestion about Macaulay's classics I discussed with C.P.T★. last night. We can neither of us remember which of us resigned the Latin classics – we only remember we both thought they ought to go to you. We both now think *your* suggestion excellent, that either Trinity or Wallington might well be the ultimate destination of the Macaulay classics. And we both think Trinity would be best, as more classical scholars will always be assembled there. His journals which I gave to the College have already been much studied there and future students of Macaulay are sure to go to the Trinity Library. Failing that, Wallington in N.T. hands would be a permanent resting place.

As to your very kind suggestion about leaving the Greek to Humphry for his life, may I ask him when he comes here in a few days and let you know what he says? I will do so unless I hear from you again.

Yrs ever,
George Trevelyan.

Dearest love to Bessie.

★Charles Philips Trevelyan (GMT's brother).

On the destination of the Greek classics.

Hallington Hall,
Newcastle-on-Tyne.
Aug. 12, 1936.

Dear Bob,

I have been talking to Humphry and I think our joint feeling is that if you feel disposed to leave the *Greek* classics (*not* the Latin classics) to him for his life he would think it very kind and highly appreciate it. If circumstances rendered it inconvenient to him to house them, he could make them over at once to Trinity (or Wallington according as you had decided). Otherwise they would go there on his death. He does care a good deal about them.

Yrs. ever
George.

My dear love to Bessie.

1938

'Janet and I are Chamberlainites'.

Garden Corner,
West Road,
Cambridge
Oct. 18, 1938.

Dear Bob,

Thank you very much for your kind letter. I am glad you like the little book. You are right: I kept off the 'high lights' purposely, partly because there is not room to develop them on so small a canvass, partly not to attempt to rival Macaulay because it would be a failure as rivalry, and I was anxious to strike a different note from Macaulay, to secure confidence for my general views, which as you see are not really very different from Macaulay's after all! For on the big impersonal issues he was right.

I am much concerned about Allen and sincerely hope Switzerland will give him some happiness, – and some health. Glad to hear better news of Bessie. Janet and I are Chamberlainites.

Yrs ever
G.M.T.

P.S. Thanks very much for the corrections. How many misprints one always misses! V. glad to see you when you come here: please stay here.

1939

Inviting Bob to Cambridge.

Garden Corner,
West Road,
Cambridge.
Feb. 15, 1939.

Dear Bob,

I sent a letter yesterday to you at Shiffolds to be forwarded, expressing my deep concern at your report from Rome of Allen's health. Today I have your p.c. from Switzerland and write to you direct, so this letter may arrive first.

We can gladly put you up any day between March 6 and 11 – only if possible choose a day other than the 10th, because Janet and I have to be in London till after dinner on that evening for her Play Centre Show though even that night you could have a (solitary) dinner, and bed. But on March 6, 7, 8, 9 or 11th we shall be free – and if you like will get tickets for the Gr Play for all 3 of us. Best of all could you come on Sat. 11 and stay the weekend. That will be the last night of the Play – we must in that case get seats as soon as poss. so please reply at once.

Yrs ever,
George.

On the eve of World War II.

Garden Corner,
West Road,
Cambridge.
Aug. 29, 1939.

Dear Bob,

Before this unredeemed calamity falls on us all and on all we value, I should like to send a word of fraternal sympathy and love to you and Bessie. Allen, dear man, is well out of it and I wish I was. Both our statesmen and our people have made mistake after mistake ever since the armistice. But there is no use harping on the obvious.

I am what they call a civil 'intelligence officer' in the Regional (East Anglia) office for civil defence – A.R.P. – and Janet is doing work for the reception of refugee children and their out of school time, as her London Play Centres will close. She will be much more useful than me. She sends her dear love.

We came down here a few days ago, from Hallington.

Your affectionate brother
George.

'We ought not to have guaranteed Poland'.

> Garden Corner,
> West Road,
> Cambridge.
> Oct. 4, 1939.

Dear Bob,

I have seen Roberts and he would like to hear your proposals, provided you are ready to foot the bill. They are not in a position to take financial risks. Otherwise they are carrying on as usual tho' of course with a reduced staff and with the possibility of losing still more staff as men are called up, so no promise can be made as to date of publication. But he likes printing for you and likes your books.

Part of the answer I think rather what you say; the other part I think it's no good breaking off now and it would only prepare a vast fleet of submarines against us. I am more inclined to think we ought not to have guaranteed Poland than that we can break off now. But I am agnostic and have no clear opinion. On the whole I think the only chance for Europe including ourselves to escape utter ruin would be for the U.S.A. to take a part in negotiating peace – but she won't, or at least she won't guarantee it.

The last thing Edward Grey said to me in the few weeks between the Nazi revolution and his death was, 'I see no hope for the world'. There is less now. One half of me suffers horribly, the other half is detached, because the 'world' that is threatened is not my world, which died years ago. I am a mere survivor. Life has been a great gift for which I am grateful, tho' I would gladly give it back now.

My dearest love to you and Bessie, always your affectionate brother

> George.

On Bob's writings.

Garden Corner,
West Road,
Cambridge.
Oct. 20, 1939.

Dear Bob,

Thank you very much indeed for your splendid Vol. II. It will join Dante (*Inferno*), Shakespeare Boccaccio, and P.G Wodehouse in the task of 'propping, in these bad days, my mind'.

Yours ever affectionately,
George.

P.S. I reopen the letter to say that I have just read '*A Custom of Thrace*'. It is very fine. The *last* page of the book is very fine indeed. Let us leave it all at that.

1940

On World War II.

Garden Corner,
West Road,
Cambridge.
Feb. 4, 1940.

Dear Bob,

Swanton's book will be useful to me and is certainly very good 'mixed feeding'. Thank you very much for the loan. I am using a good many items out of it and will return it when done. He has scholarly scientific knowledge on many sides.

I have much sympathy with C.R.B.* and until the war began I was in general agreement with him. But I doubt whether now an appeal for a Conference with no terms agreed on in general beforehand would do anything but make the French and neutrals think we were giving in; and I fear Hitler is by no means ready to consider the sort of terms C.R.B. suggests. But a time may come when such a step will be right.

Yrs ever,
George.

*C.R. Buxton

On World War II.

Garden Corner,
West Road,
Cambridge.
July 12, 1940.

Dear Bob,

I know that Tovey's death will be a grief and loss to you of no ordinary kind and Janet and I send our sincerest sympathy. For him – I fear we live in days when anyone of our generation who dies is lucky. I never had any real hope for the world after this war broke out, but it is all going even worse than I feared. But I can see no course for us now but to fight on for it is not an enemy from whom we can get terms or agreement.

The combination of defying great enemy powers without arming as they were armed has been a hideous and fatal folly. But we must now make the best of it.

Yours ever,
George.

Help for an Italian anti-fascist.

> Hallington Hall,
> Newcastle-on-Tyne.
> Aug. 6, 1940.

Dear Bob,

I am here for a few days, arranging about the taking over of this house by the Air Force for the duration of the war. It is not quite settled but I think will be. It is a small thing in this doomsday, but I should have minded a year ago, for I doubt if I am ever likely to be able to live here again, and I love it.

I enclose a letter of Gilbert Murray's. I was appealed to help Mrs Vivanto and wrote to the Home Office about her husband and two sons. But I do not know him personally, as I believe you do well. Do you feel inclined to write a letter of the kind suggested in the first para. of Gilbert Murray's letter? It would be used by her in the endeavour to secure the release of her husband and the boy now in the Isle of Man.

You could either send it direct to her (Meriden Bungalow,

> Boar's Hill
> Oxford)

or to Gilbert Murray★, or if you like to me when I would add a letter of my own about the known anti-Fascist fame of the family (Lauro de Bosis' death etc.) and send it on.

I shall probably be here for another week.

> Yours ever affectionately,
> George

I hardly dare to think of Holland – and Bessie. The world is a worse nightmare than imagination could have devised. Every evil seems to have occurred.

★Gilbert Murray (1866–1957); Regius professor of Greek, Oxford,1908–36; O.M., 1941; major works: *Rise of the Greek Epic* (1907); *Euripides and his Age* (1913).

Appointed Master of Trinity College Cambridge.

1.

Garden Corner,
West Road,
Cambridge

Private

Sept. 27, 1940.

Dear Bob,

I want to tell you and Bessie before you see it in the papers, that I am to be Master of Trinity. Do not tell anyone else till it is public. I have the Prime Minister's letter today and shall answer, accepting, on Sunday. The Fellows are very anxious I should accept, the more so as they do not know whom Winston would appoint if I refused, and there are some people not without claims whom they don't want. Everyone concerned has been so kind about it that I can't leave them in the lurch. Janet will be the loser, but she is clear that I cannot refuse, and she is being very good about it.

I did not want to be Master, and if peace had continued I doubt if anything would have made me accept. But I have no other war work that is of any real importance; Hallington has been taken over by the R.A.F. and I don't suppose I shall ever be able to afford to live there again; and as everyone seems to want me to do this I must try.

That the crash of civilization should have landed me in the beautiful old Lodge with its peaceful old-world traditions of Montagu Butler and Whewell and Bentley*, is a tragi-comic irony. But we shall not move in there till January and meanwhile it may be destroyed by a bomb!

Yrs affectionately
George.

*Richard Bentley (1662–1742), appointed Master of Trinity,1700; William Whewell (1794–1866),appointed 1841; Henry Montagu Butler (1833–1918); appointed 1886.

2.

Garden Corner,
West Road
Cambridge.
Oct. 25, 1940.

Dear Bob,

I have now got the King's Letters Patent as Master of Trinity, and on Nov. 16 I shall be admitted as Master and begin to perform his functions. But we shall not get into the Lodge till January as there is much to be done there in the way of painting etc. and labour and materials are scarce. When we are in, I hope we shall soon get you as a visitor. I don't think it is worth while your coming to my admission ceremony, as it has to be done with maimed rights, and trains are awful and all Cambridge houses are crowded up with billettees and refugees. No colleges have been hit yet and so far we are fairly quiet. I hope you are all of you all right.

Yours ever affectionately
George.

On reading Bob's *Horace.*

> Garden Corner,
> West Road.
> Cambridge.
> Dec. 8, 1940

Dear Bob,

Thank you very much for your *Horace.* I have read it all with great enjoyment, but most of all I liked the two dialogues at the end. I am so glad you think Horace was really like that. It was my idea of him and your much greater knowledge and thought on the subject enables me to keep the picture. It is moreover a beautiful piece of writing. Did you ever read John Buchan's *Augustus,* I wonder. I think it is so good if true, and the ancient historians say it is true and accurate. I go to Wallington for a week at Christmas, Hallington being occupied by the R.A.F., while Janet visits Humphry and Mary respectively. After that we have a hectic fortnight of more house moving and settling into the Lodge, where the workmen are very busy now. If Hitler doesn't put in a bomb, it will certainly look better inside than it has looked for many a long year. Best love to Bessie.

> Yours affectionately,
> George.

'I find great comfort in great poetry'.

Wallington,
Dec. 29, 1940

Dear Bob,

Thank you very much indeed for your 'letter to Joan', which I thought very good and wise and beautiful. I think it is great to be able to express at all what one feels or tries to feel in this utter dissolution of all things that are good. One has to be both poet and philosopher to do so and you are both. I am neither, creatively, but I find great comfort in great poetry. I have been reading *Lear* twice over, and also Bradley★ on *Lear* and Granville Barker† on *Lear* both as fine pieces of expository criticism as any I know on any great work of genius, and complementary to each other, written from two different points of view – the study and the stage.

Lear has a 'happy ending' – without Tate's help. All the bad people are killed and most of the good left to rule the land. In the real world this does not happen.

Your affectionate brother,

George.

People here seem friendly and happy; Molly much happier.

★Andrew Cecil Bradley (1851–1935), one of the greatest English critics of Shakespeare; professor of poetry, Oxford, 1901-6.
†Harley Granville-Barker (1877–1946); actor, producer, dramatist, and critic.

Helping a displaced academic.

> The Master's Lodge,
> Trinity College,
> Cambridge.
> Jan. 24, 1941.

Dear Bob,

We are doing what we can for Daskaloff, whom we both liked. The University authorities are trying to fit him in as a research student and I hope it will go all right. Could you forward enclosed to Max B. as I do not know his address.

> Yrs ever affectionately,
> G.M. Trevelyan.

We are gradually getting the Lodge repaired, and repainted. It is a slow but amusing business. Daskaloff gave us an account of Bessie's eyes that might have been worse.

1941

Inviting Max Beerbohm* to give a series of lectures at Trinity.

1.

24th January, 1941.

Sir Max Beerbohm.

Dear Sir Max Beerbohm,

I am writing at the behest of the Council of Trinity College to ask whether you could honour us by giving the Clark Lectures in this College, open to the University, either in the Lent or Summer Term of 1942. Our common friend Desmond MacCarthy and other distinguished literary critics have given them in the past. You could choose any literary subject that you liked. The lectures should be not less than six in number and not more than eight. The stipend is £150. Of course in these days everything must be provisional and circumstances may render it necessary to postpone the event. But we should value the chance of having you more than the certainty of having others.

Yours sincerely,
G.M. Trevelyan.

P.S. As I do not know your present address and I believe you are living near my brother Bob, I am sending this to him to forward.

---

*Sir Henry Maximilian Beerbohm (1872–1956); author & cartoonist; dramatic critic *Saturday Review*, 1898–1910.

2.

The Master's Lodge,
Trinity College,
Cambridge.
7th February, 1941.

R.C. Trevelyan Esq.

Dear Bob,
I enclose a copy of the letter which I sent on January 24th to Max Beerbohm through you. You wrote to say you had been good enough to forward it. I have not heard from him yet. It is possible that he is still making up his mind. But I am also told that he does not much care about answering letters. I wonder if you could by any chance find out whether he got the letter and if so what his views are.

Yours ever,
G.M. Trevelyan.

If you don't care to undertake the mission, send the copy of the letter back to me and I will write to him again in a few days' time.

3.

The Master's Lodge,
Trinity College,
Cambridge.
Feb. 14, 1941.

R.C. Trevelyan Esq.,
The Shiffolds,
Holmbury St. Mary,
Nr. Dorking.

Dear Bob,

Max B. has answered my letter with a very delightful one of his own, tho' as I feared he will not accept the invitation. If you intervened to extract the answer, thank you very much.

Yrs ever,
G.M.T.

We can now put you up for the night if ever you come to Cam.

A gift to the National Trust.

The Master's Lodge,
Trinity College,
Cambridge.

<u>Confidential</u>   8th April, 1941.

Dear Bob,

I am sending this letter to you and to Aunt Annie, Humphry and Mary.

My brother Charles, largely on the advice of myself and of his wife, has decided to hand over the Wallington house and estate as a gift to the National Trust at once. He will reserve a life interest for himself in its management. After his death he requests the National Trust to allow Molly to be the tenant of the house at a nominal rent and if she dies or declines the tenancy, then one of his children. He also requests the National Trust to vest the management of the estate for the National Trust in one of his children. The National Trust officers have agreed to get a resolution passed by the Executive Body of the Trust declaring their intention to do this. Although doing that, they cannot be legally bound to do so without incurring death duties. But the Trust will certainly fulfil its promise.

I entirely approve of this arrangement. As Executor of his will I urged it, because under his will there would have been death duties to pay which will now be altogether avoided. In this way a very considerable, though of course indefinite, amount of money will be saved to the family. For the National Trust has now agreed to accept the estate without the sum of money which Charles had previously left them in his will to pay death duties. That is no longer necessary.

There is, therefore, no doubt that if the Wallington estate is to go to the National Trust at all, this is the best way and possibly the only way to do it, for who knows how much money there will be or what death duties will be at the time of his death?

Of course it is possible to take the view that the house and estate ought not to be left to the National Trust at all. Prior to the war I did not take a decided view on this question, but I clearly perceived that my brother was determined to do it and therefore became his Executor in order to make it as easy as possible for all concerned, and I am bound to say that the circumstances of the war and the probable state of things after the war make me more favourably disposed towards the plan in its general aspect. For I am now perfectly certain that it would be financially impossible for George or anyone else to continue to run the estate burdened with death duties without their selling the treasures of Wallington or large parts of the estate or both, and this would be increasingly the case from generation to generation. If, therefore it is an important object to preserve the amenities and treasures of Wallington and the management of the estate as a whole, the National Trust seems to me the only possible way of doing it.

I confess I think George has been hardly treated in not being more consulted and given a more definite place in the arrangement. But in old days he showed no interest in Wallington, and his father is absolutely determined (in theory) not to treat him as an 'eldest son'. This being so, I am certain the new arrangement is much the best thing for George, for there will be more money, and the likelihood of his being ultimately the tenant of the house and/or the manager of the estate is at least as good as it was before.

Yours ever affectionately,
G.M.T.

On Bob's *Dream.*

> The Master's Lodge,
> Trinity College,
> Cambridge.
> Dec. 7, 1941.

Dear Bob,

I love your *Dream*. It is individual to you; and the form is interesting and beautiful, and has a smack of Piers Plowman in it. Indeed it is liker to Piers Plowman than to anything else I can recall.

The more I look at Max's portrait of you the more I admire it. I suppose there are not spare copies I could buy? We are hoping to see you here next term. Janet and I are going to try to spend a Xmas fortnight at Hallington – in the empty gardener's house. The big house is being converted into a hospital, after having served for six months as an R.A.F. centre.

We are going to Wallington for Xmas Day itself.

> Best love to Bessie,
> Yours ever,
> George.

A personal note to Bob.

The Master's Lodge,
Trinity College,
Cambridge.
Dec. 14, 1941.

Dear Bob,
I am most delighted to have the other copies of Max's portrait. Thank you very much indeed. We have Desmond staying here this weekend which is delightful. He is reading H's *Goethe*★ and will review it. He admires it and I am glad you do too. Janet and I are going to Hallington from Dec. 19 to Jan. 6 to live in the gardener's house – the large house is being turned into a hospital, after having ceased to be an R.A.F. scientific base.

We look forward greatly to a visit from you next term.
Our best Christmas wishes to you all.

Yrs ever,
George.

★Humphry Trevelyan, *Goethe & the Greeks* (1941).

1942

On reading Bob's *Aftermath* poems.

> The Master's Lodge,
> Trinity College,
> Cambridge.
> March 30, 1942.

Dear Bob,

Thank you very much for *Aftermath*. I am glad you have salvaged so many poems of which I am so fond. The family connection with Longmans has been by purest accident a bad business for both of us. Personally I don't much care. One has got past bothering whether anyone reads one's books or not, in this night of time. I have no more desire for continued existence as an author than for life after death. But I have begun chattering about myself, when what I want to say is how much I love these poems of yours which you have here republished. The Geoffrey Youngs★ are staying in the Lodge for a few days, in process of moving into a house nearby. It is good to have them again in Cambridge. Come down here some time in the summer days. We hope to get to Hallington for ten days at Easter – living in the gardener's cottage. The Hall has now begun again as a hospital. We shall see more of it and its inmates than when it was an R.A.F. affair.

> Love to Bessie.

I hope you have good news of Julian from Egypt.

> Yrs. ever,
> G.M.T.

Aubrey and Lina Waterfield's son has been killed in Malta.

★Geoffrey Winthrop Young (1876–1958), British mountaineer; war correspondent (1914); wrote poetry; GMT's lifelong friend.

1943

On the consequences of Lady Russell knitting during her husband's lectures.

The Master's Lodge,
Trinity College,
Cambridge.
January 25th 1943.

Dear Bob,

Thanks for yours of January 22nd. I can tell you a little more about Bertie, though not very much. His lectureship was not for a regular university but was being given in the Barnes Foundation for art students. Albert Barnes is a very eccentric millionaire who has violently quarrelled with the Philadelphia University next door. Bertie, I understand, took the precaution of getting a very definite covenant from him before he began giving the lectures, and now intends to sue him for breach of contract. Barnes is so very odd a man that the catastrophe is not to be wondered at. The actual quarrel seems to have arisen because the present Lady Russell insisted on knitting during her husband's lectures and would not give over when Barnes very unnecessarily told her to. Bertie also thinks that his defence of the Cripps* policy in India against anti-British criticism has had something to do with the quarrel.

It is rather early to say what could be done for him if he had to come back here. Clearly there would be no political difficulties. But, as you know, all except 'technical' that is scientific, students are being prevented from coming up or staying at the Universities in this country for the remainder of the war, and that fact together with Bertie's age would make it impossible to engage him as an ordinary lecturer at Cambridge, and I suppose at any other university. But of course something extraordinary might be devised. I should think that he would get the largest audiences in London, but at this moment I cannot say more.

Thanks for your congratulations about Thomas Arnold.† I am so glad that you are getting better, and I hope that when you are better still, and when the weather is better too, you and Bessie will be able to come here some time in next term.

Yours affectionately,
G.M. Trevelyan

*Sir Stafford Cripps (1889–1952); statesman and lawyer; Labour MP, 1931–1950
†Thomas Arnold (1795–1842), headmaster of Rugby, English scholar; works include: *History of Rome* (3 vols.,1838–43); father of Matthew Arnold (1822–88), the poet; granddaughter, Mary (Mrs. Ward), whose daughter, Jane, wife of GMT.

On the writings of Basil Willie.

The Master's Lodge,
Trinity College,
Cambridge.
March 30. (later)

Dear Bob,

Since I posted my other letter to you I have been reading *Aftermath*, and to my great delight found a number of poems quite new to me, chiefly dated 1940 or 1941. I like them as much as any.

I wonder if you ever read a book called *The Seventeenth Century Background* by Basil Willie, a Cambridge don, which I think is the history book that has most interested me of recent years. It is about the philosophy, science and poetry of that period, leading up to the 18th cent. and Wordsworth. There is also another book of his, more recent called *The Eighteenth Century Background*; also very good. I was reminded to tell you of it when I was reading 'The Spirit of Man' in *Aftermath*. I will show them you when you come here.

Yrs. ever
G.M.T.

On an edition of *Abinger Chronicle*.

The Master's Lodge,
Trinity College,
Cambridge.
June 8th 1943

Dear Bob,

I congratulate you heartily on Volume IV No. 2 of the *Abinger Chronicle*. I think it is almost the only example I have come across of a magazine in which I really liked all the prose and all the verse in a particular number. Naturally your description of the Middle Pond came very close to my love and memory.

Give our dear love to Bessie.

Yours ever,
G.M. Trevelyan.

On Bob's writings.

The Master's Lodge,
Trinity College,
Cambridge.
July 13, 1943.

Dear Bob,

I liked your reminiscences of old Thornton very much, and your defence of rough shooting is the best I have read. Indeed your last article was a delightful piece of writing, and you can imagine how I liked it. It brought back the past indeed.

Janet and I are much concerned to hear that you are losing your servants and are very anxious to hear that you and Bessie will be able to make a shift.

Yours ever,
G.M.T.

'I am very, very glad that you have a grandson'.

Robin Ghyll★

As from
The Master's Lodge,
Trinity College,
Cambridge.
Aug. 26, 1945.

Dear Bob,

Janet and I were indeed delighted to get Bessie's most kind letter about this happy event. It only reached us this morning up at Robin Ghyll; but I am coming back to Trinity on Monday and Janet in a few days.

I am very, very glad that you have got a grandson. The losses that you and Bessie sustained early in life were cruel. The memory of them makes me feel the more deeply thankful for this. Please send on the enclosed to Julian.

Yours ever
George.

Certainly the younger generation of our old Wallington family is filling up.

★Family cottage in Langdale.

1944

Twin grandsons are born in the Lodge at Trinity.

The Master's Lodge,
Trinity College,
Cambridge.
April 2, 1944.

Dear Bob and Bessie,

Two twin grandsons were born in the Lodge yesterday, to be called George Macaulay and Humphrey Bennett. They and Molly are very well, I am glad to say.

Tomorrow Janet and I are going to Hallington to stay 10 days in the gardener's cottage as usual in war time.

I hope we shall see something of you here this summer.

Yrs ever
G.M.T.

Bertrand Russell's whereabouts.

The Master's Lodge,
Trinity College,
Cambridge.
June 27th 1944.

Dear Bessie,

I am glad you like Veronica Wedgwood's WILLIAM. Bertie Russell is at present living at the Clifton Place Hotel, Sidmouth, South Devon. His wife and son are with him there and I am afraid the son is not very well but recovering. He himself will actually be here at Trinity for day after tomorrow, Thursday, and Friday nights, but I should advise you to write to Sidmouth as posts are slow, even if you write here also.

I am very much interested in Ralph Vaughan Williams' offer to the National Trust.

Yours ever,
G.M. Trevelyan.

Life at Hallington Hall.

Hallington Hall,
Newcastle-on-Tyne.
Aug. 3, 1944.

Dear Bob,

Please find and deal with enclosed. Janet and I are up here in the gardener's cottage for August. The hospital in the Hall is full of convalescent wounded from Normandy – nice fellows who like the quiet of the place. It is sunless still except at intervals. Charles and Molly seem well and happy.

I take this opportunity of saying to you how much I thought about old days when I read of Tom Moore's★ death. There was a nice article about him by Desmond in the *Sunday Times*.

Don't bother to answer this.

I hope you will shortly get a copy of my new book (written indeed some years ago) which I told Longmans to send you. Best love to Bessie.

Yrs ever
G.M.T.

★Thomas Moore (1870–1944), English poet, critic and wood-engraver (brother of G.E. Moore, the Cambridge philosopher).

On Bob's writings.

The Master's Lodge,
Trinity College
Cambridge.
September 15th 1944.

Dear Bob,

Thanks very much for yours of September 13th. I am very glad that Bessie is enjoying your reading of the book to her.

I am very glad that you say that you must try to write some more in the general style of 'Notes on Poetry and Prose'. I thought that particular section very good indeed. It seemed to me a method of criticism and appreciation peculiar to yourself and based on much more of real scholarship and real thought about, and love of, the poems in question than is usual in literary criticism. I should like more of it from you, perhaps in a separate book.

Yours ever,
G.M. Trevelyan.

On Churchill's obstinacy.

The Master's Lodge,
Trinity College,
Cambridge.
Christmas Day, 1944

Dear Bob,

Thank you very much for the *Eclogues* and *Georgics*. I had already seen and admired the Introductions which you read me, and I am now browsing with great pleasure in the translations. You are certainly at the head of translators of the Classics now. Nothing gives me greater pleasure than the general recognition of the excellence of your work, rather late in life but very marked, of *all* your work I mean, not merely the translations.

My dearest love to Bessie. In all the bitter scene two things specially grieve me, Holland and Greece. The plight of Holland is not our fault, except for our share in the whole business, but Greece I think has been badly muddled by Churchill whose obstinacy is sometimes a blessing but sometimes the reverse.

As to the future, hope is better than prophecy. All prophets, even the best informed, seem usually to be wrong.

I am so glad about Leith Hill Place. You will find Wedgwood a delightful neighbour.

Yours ever
George.

1945

On the Labour election victory.

Hallington
Newcastle on Tyne.

The Master's Lodge,
Trinity College,
Cambridge.
July 31, 1945.

Dear Bob,

Thanks for yours of July 27. I return Mr Taylor's letter and will leave the matter in your hands.

We are here till Aug. 20, then the Lakes for a few days, then Cambridge again. Letters will always be forwarded from Cambridge.

I like the result of the election, I think, though of course things may turn out badly yet, as they often do. But I don't see how a purely Conservative govt. could in the present conditions have turned out well. And tho' I agree with the Liberals well enough, I should greatly fear that if they had held the balance we should have had long delay in getting any govt. and then have got a weak one, – very fatal in the present state of the world. The Labour leaders have now had some very realistic experience in government which they so sorely lacked before 1940. I hope they will nationalize the mines.

Dearest love to Bessie. Hoping to see you at Cam. next term.

Yrs ever
George.

1946

A note to Bessie.

> The Master's Lodge,
> Trinity College,
> Cambridge.
> Feb. 20, 1946.

Dear Bessie,

Thank you very much for your most kind letter. I am so glad you and Bob liked my lecture. Yes, it is very good that the Ralph Wedgwoods are living at Leith Hill Place. I cannot imagine better neighbours for you, and they regard your neighbourhood as one of attractions of the place, where they are most happy.

I had a very nice sight of Bob yesterday and a talk with him about the poets, always most refreshing.

> Yours ever affectionately,
> G.M. Trevelyan.

On reading Bob's *Oedipus*.

> The Master's Lodge,
> Trinity College,
> Cambridge.
> Ap. 11, 1946.

Dear Bob,

It was very good of you to send us the *Oedipus C*. I am reading it with delight and interest, the more so as I never before read it in Greek or in English. Janet greatly looks forward to reading it; she is the best Grecian of us two.

You certainly are having a great harvest in your old age – like Sophocles. I am more played out as a history writer than you as a poet. Best love to Bessie.

> Yrs ever
> G.M.T.

1947

'Calming and strengthening effect' of Bob's poems.

The Master's Lodge,
Trinity College,
Cambridge.
July 6, 1947.

Dear Bob,

Thanks very much for '*From the Shiffolds*' which I have been reading with joy – some old friends and others new to me. Your mind and attitude to life and imaginings have a calming and strengthening effect on me as no other present-day poet has. In the matter of writing I am much more *rude donatus* than you are in spite of our years difference. I much look forward to the Groves dinner.

Yrs ever
G.M.T.

Dearest love to Bessie.

1948

GMT on his *Autobiography*.

1.

The Master's Lodge,
Trinity College,
Cambridge.
Dec. 20, 1948.

Dear Bob,

Thank you very much for sending me your usual Christmas present *From the Shiffolds*.

I am going up tomorrow night, after the Entrance Scholarship Election meetings, to Hallington for Christmas and New Year. Humphry and Molly and their 5 children will be there. Janet is not coming as the northern winter is not very good for her, tho' on the whole she has kept fairly well this term. I hope to have my *Autobiography and other essays* out in May this year and will send you a copy. It will probably be the last new book I shall ever bring out.

I have just been reading again Maitland's *Life of Leslie Stephen*. The first few chapters are rather dull perhaps, but after that I think it is one of the very best biographies in our language.

Yrs ever
G.M.T.

Dearest love to Bessie.

1949

2.

The Master's Lodge,
Trinity College,
Cambridge.
May 20th 1949.

Dear Bessie,

Thank you very much for your kind letter. I value your approval of my *Auto-biography* very highly. Several of my friends and family have told me that it is not long enough, but I note that your literary sense causes you to suspend judgement on that point. I think I knew what I was about. After all, one's personal friends and relations are more interested in one, and in one's very mild adventures in life, than the general public can be. I have really said all about myself that I think the public has a right to know or would wish to know. And if I have said it in a way to win your approval I think it is all right.

I am glad we had Dr Bluth to see Janet. I do not feel at all certain that the tablets he has given her to take will make any marked improvement. But it is a great thing to know that so great a specialist as he agrees with our Dr. Simpson. They both thought highly of each other.

Dearest love to Bob.

Yours affectionately,
G.M. Trevelyan

I think I made it clear that my admission to shout in the School Choir was by favour (of Sandilands) not, by merit!!

3.

The Master's Lodge,
Trinity College,
Cambridge.
25th May 1949.

Dear Bob,

Thanks for your very kind letter. As you and Bessie and Desmond MacCarthy all think my *Autobiography* was all right and not too short, I feel that I have managed that rather delicate operation satisfactorily, and I am glad you like the rest of the book.

I am afraid I cannot say that Janet is really getting better though she is no worse. I am glad that we had Dr. Bluth: he and our Dr. Simpson quite agreed over the case.

Your affectionate brother,
G.M. Trevelyan.

On Bob's translation of the classics.

The Master's Lodge,
Trinity College,
Cambridge.
July 13, 1949.

Dear Bob,

Thank you very much for your delightful translations. I have read them through with pleasure. The Catullus originals I know well, but not the others except partly the Leopardi.

Those Italian Folk Songs at the very end are remarkable and quite unknown to me. We are going to Hallington on Friday, a tiresome journey for Janet who gets no better. But we shall both be glad to be up there. I hope we shall see you there when you come north.

Best love to Bessie.

Yours ever affectionately,
G.M.T.

1951

GMT to Desmond MacCarthy about Bob.

The Master's Lodge,
Trinity College,
Cambridge.
Ap. 1, 1951.

Dear Desmond

Your article about Bob personally, in today's S.T., is lovely. Nothing would be truer or more beautiful. I had a very good week of seeing him in the nursing home here after you left us. He talked so clearly and well about books after he was unable to be clear about anything else. It is a merciful release. I do not pity old people who die – particularly nowadays. How many hours good reading he had in his life.

I think the poetry he wrote in middle and later life was better than the poetry of his youth when he was obsessed by theories of what poetry ought to be and so missed expressing *himself*. It was both then his strength and his weakness that he was a learned poet. If he had not been indeed, he could not have written his translations which all scholars praise.

There are 2 other poets of *our* generation who have been overlooked. I wonder if you know the work of either. I mean Geoffrey Young (who has got fame as a mountaineer and a writer on mountains but been overlooked as a poet of great imaginable power). And Margaret Cropper, whose Westmorland poems *The Broken Hearth Stone, Little Mary Crosby* and the *End of the Road* seem to me much greater than the Dorset and other dialect poems which the world has acclaimed. I wonder if you know the volumes I have mentioned.

Yours ever
G.M.T.

To Bessie about the destination of Macaulay's classics.

> Hallington Hall
> Newcastle-on-Tyne.
> till Oct. 15. Then
> 23 West Road, Cambridge.
> Oct. 10, 1951.

Dear Bessie,

Thank you very much for your kind letter. I am so very glad about the Macaulay Classics. I am sure nothing better could be found as a permanent home. In a library of the size and peculiarity of Trinity they will be less lost and more known of than in a very large library.

I am so glad you are, for the present, staying on at the Shiffolds.

Best love from us both.

> Yrs ever,
> G.M. Trevelyan

Index

Acton, Lord, 27
Amos, Sir Maurice, 18–19, 36, 42, 82–3
Angel, Sir Norman, 88
Arnold, E.P., 1
Arnold, Matthew, 45, 143
Arnold, Thomas, 57, 143
Asquith, 89

Baker, Philip Wilbraham, 4
Barnes, Albert, 143
Barnett, Lionel David, 27
Beerbohm, Sir Henry Maximilian,
    134–37
Bell, Sir Hugh, 94
Bell, Mary, 94
Bell, Maurice, 63
Bentley, Richard, 130
Berenson, Bernard, 31, 83
Blacket, Sir William, ix
Bottomley, Horatio William, 79
Bourchier, E., ix
Bowen, Edward, ix, 4, 48
Bradley, Andrew Cecil, 133
Bradley, Robert William, 11
Butler, Henry Montagu, 130
Buxton, Charles Roden, 4, 42, 127
Buxton, Earl Sydney Charles, 20, 22, 26
Byron, Lord, 20

Cannadine, David, xiv, xv
Carlyle, 82
Cavour, 68
Churchill, Winston, xiii, 130
Clarendon, 80
Cripps, Sir Stafford, 143
Cropper, Margaret, 156
Crowdy, James, 15

Daskaloff, 134
De Quincey, Thomas, 19

De Wet, C.R., 56
Derby, Lord, 42
Dreyfus, 35

Elliot, Edward Hugh, 9–10, 20

Farquhar, Hobart Brooks, 7, 10
Fleming, R., 71
Franklin, Sir John, x

Garibaldi, xii, 61, 63
Gaskell, Philip, xvi
Geikie, Roderick, 14
George V, 12
Geyl, Pietr, 102
Giolitti, Giovanni, 91
Gooch, George Peabody, 18, 36
Granville-Barker, Harley, 133
Grey, Sir Edward, 71, 89

Hardy, 61
Heine, 35
Hernon, J.M., xii, 17
Hicks, Frederick Cyril, 9
Homer, 25
Housman, Alfred Edward, 119
Hunter, Peter, xvi
Huxley, Sir Julian, 70

Jackson, Sir Francis, 91, 97
Jebb, Sir Richard, 49
Jones, Herbert, 68

Keats, 20
Kruger, Paul, 56

Lee, Vernon, 76
Lowes Dickinson, G., 36, 45, 49

Macaulay, Hannah Moore, ix

Macaulay, Lord, ix, xii, 2, 109–10, 121, 123, 157

MacCarthy, Desmond, xv, 18, 60, 67, 135, 155–56

Machiavelli, Niccolo, 91

Maitland, Frederic, 18, 153

Manin, Daniele, 100

Marlborough, Lord, 113

Mayor, Robin, 57

Mazzini, Giuseppe, 91

McKitterick, David, xvi

Meredith, George, 53, 72

Milton, 33, 93

Moore, George Edward, 18–20, 24, 27, 49, 147

Moore, Thomas, 58, 147

Moorman, John, xi, 111

Moorman, Mary, xiv, 2, 6, 18, 111, 132, 138

Morel, Edmund, 88

Murray, Gilbert, 129

Nelson Gay, H., xii

Petrarch, Francesco, 94

Philips, Anna Maria, 6

Phillips, Robert Needham, ix

Plato, 25–6

Ponsonby, Arthur, 92

Princess Mary, 12

Robson, Robert, xvi

Rome, Claud Stuart, 10–11, 15

Rosebery, Lord, 55

Rossetti, D.G., 75

Rothenstein, Sir William, 77

Rothschild, 11

Rowse, A.L., xvi

Ruskin, 8, 46

Russell, Bertrand, 18, 36, 42, 60, 82, 143, 146

Sandilands, Harold Richard, 4, 10, 15–16

Scott, Sir Walter, 19

Seton-Watson, 90

Shakespeare, 2, 127

Shelley, 25

Sidgwick, Henry, 34, 43, 71

Smith, John Alexander, 71

Stow, Arthur Rigby, 9

Sykes, Sir Frederick, 95

Taggart, John m., 36, 42, 44–5, 71

Tagore, Sir Rabindranath, 78

Tait, James, xii

Tennyson, Lord, ix, x

Thycydides, 80

Tovey, Donald, xiv

Tregoning, Arthur Langford, 7, 15

Trevelyan, Sir Charles Edward, ix, xiv, 1, 17, 50–52, 57, 81–2, 94, 121

Trevelyan, Elizabeth (Bessie), xvi, 46, 50–1, 55–6, 58–60, 63, 66, 69–70, 90, 105, 121–22, 153–54, 157

Trevelyan, George Macaulay (GMT):
  Biographical references, ix–xvi
  Letters from: to Robert Trevelyan (Bob): childhood letters, 1–3; life at Harrow, 4–16; at Cambridge: new acquaintances, 18–20; 24–5; love for poetry, 21; in Switzerland, 22–3; Trinity Fellowships, 27; GMT's first book, 29, 34; visit to Sicily, 32–3; Cambridge gossip, 36; reflections after reading Bob's novel, 37; the countryside, 40–41; on liking sonnets, 41; student life, 42, about writing, 44; on reading Wordsworth, 45; Ruskin, 46; on his house master at Harrow, 48, on mutual relationships within the Trevelyan family, 50–52; the Boer War, 54
  Admiration for Bob's writings: 37, 55, 61–2, 66–7, 76, 93, 96, 98, 101, 102, 104, 106, 118–19, 127, 132, 140, 142, 151–52, 155

Thanking Bob for editorial help: 63, 68, 74, 79, 99, 103, 104, 113, 117 GMT's engagement, 57; Thomas Moore's poems, 58; disapproval of Desmond MacCarthy entering politics, 60; on Garibaldi, 61; civil servants, 63; in Italy, 70–71, 94–5; the Royal Society of Literature, 72; on Tagore & Yeats, 78; the Balkans, 80; World War I, 81–9; 91; the Finns, 92; the future of Italy, 100; appointed Regius Professor of History at Cambridge, 105; the Trevelyan library, 109, 115–16; the Macaulay journals, 110; Chamberlainites, 123; World War II, 125; 127–28; guarantee to Poland, 126; help for an Italian anti-fascist, 129; appointed Master of Trinity College, Cambridge, 130; comfort in great poetry, 133; helping a displaced academic, 134; inviting Max Beerbohm to give a series of lectures at Trinity college, 135–37; a gift to the National Trust, 138–39; on the consequences of Lady Russell knitting during her husband's lectures, 143; twin grandsons born, 146; Bertrand Russell's whereabouts, 146; Life at Hallington Hall, 147; Churchill's obstinacy, 149; the Labour election victory, 150; GMT's Autobiography, 153–55; thanking Desmond MacCarthy for his article on Bob, 156
Letters from: to Elizabeth (Bessie): 56, 59, 66, 69–70, 101–02, 108, 113–14, 151, 157
Letters to: from: Robert Trevelyan (Bob) on World War I, 82–5
Trevelyan, George Macaulay (GMT's grandson), xvi, 146
Trevelyan, Sir George Otto, ix, 1, 4, 52–7, 97, 99, 107–09, 115–16
Trevelyan Humphry (GMT's son), 101, 132, 138, 141

Trevelyan, Humphry Bennett (GMT's grandson), 146
Trevelyan, Lord Humphrey, xiv
Trevelyan, Janet Penrose, xi, 120
Trevelyan, Julian Otto, xiv, 76, 90, 92, 142
Trevelyan, Mary, xi
Trevelyan, Paul, 59, 64, 75, 128
Trevelyan, Raleigh, xvi
Trevelyan, Robert Calverley, ix, xiv, xv, 1, 31, – see under GMT (Letters)
Trevelyan, Theodore Macaulay, 53

Venizelos, E., 80
Verrall, Arthur, 29–30

Ward, Humphry, xi
Ward, Janet, xi, 57
Ward, Mary, xi, 57, 143
Warner, Townsend, ix
Waterfield, Aubrey, 142
Waterfield, Lina, 142
Webb, Beatrice, 78
Webb, Sidney, 52, 78
Wedgwood, Sir Ralph Lewis, 18–19, 20, 24, 42, 149
Wedgwood Veronica, 18, 146
Welldon, 37
Wells, H.G., 84, 88
Whewell, William, 130
Whitehead, Alfred North, 18
Will, Arnold Foster, 74, 76
William III, ix
Williams, Basil, 88
Williams, Ralph Vaughan, 18–19, 42, 146
Willie, Basil, 144
Wodehouse, P.G., 127
Wordsworth, 45, 144

Yeats, William Butler, 78
Young, Geoffrey Winthrop, 142, 156
Young, Hilton, 57